THE
NEW
DAY

An Autobiography,
Entrepreneur's Guide,
& Spiritual Primer

www.TheNewDay.org

CHARLES PAUL CURCIO

Delphi University Press

The New Day
An Autobiography, Entrepreneur's Guide, & Spiritual Primer
All Rights Reserved.
Copyright © 2012 Charles Paul Curcio
v3.0
Website: wwwTheNewDay.org

Delphi University Press
Website: www.delphiu.com

ISBN: 978-0-578-10556-7

Know Thyself

This book is dedicated to all
Spiritual Seekers, Practicing Masters,
Initiates, and Fellow Journeymen and Women
in the continuing adventure of life, love, and Spirit

Acknowledgements

I wish to acknowledge my father, Charles Paul Curcio Sr., who taught me how to work hard and be self-reliant.

To my mother, Philomena Curcio, the best person I've ever known, a great spiritual being who raised and supported seven children all by herself, and made countless numbers of people laugh, smile, and feel good about themselves.

To my children and family, who taught me how to love unconditionally, and who gave me purpose and meaning in life.

To Jim Coates who taught me more about the tire business than I really ever wanted to know.

To my Tire Kingdom friends and family for the love, success, and fond memories we all share.

To Delphi University founders and spiritual pioneers Patricia Hayes and Marshall Smith, for their tireless work and their incredible teachings and gifts of healing, spiritual understanding, and wisdom.

Also to the incredible staff of instructors at Delphi who have selflessly dedicated themselves and their lives in service to God and their fellow human beings.

To the students and graduates of Delphi University who shine their light out into the world each day, helping to make the earth a better place, and bringing love, light, and healing to all those who step upon their paths.

And to each and every spiritual being who has taken the journey and entered into the Human Idea.

And finally, I wish to acknowledge my beautiful wife and partner Kimberly Hayes Curcio, who has taught me more about love, life, the Universe, and myself than I ever dreamed possible.

Chapter List

CHAPTER ONE

Introduction

I had always wanted to tell you these things. But I couldn't begin without putting it all together myself. I have been waiting, waiting until I was ready, waiting until the time was ready, waiting until you were ready. And now in these dramatically changing times we are all ready, ready to feel, ready to experience, ready to know the truth: the truth about life, about being, about self, the way things are. The New Day has come. Some of what I share with you will be conventional and traditional wisdom. Most will not. Many things I say you will never have heard before, or never dreamed possible. Some insights will open your heart and jog your spiritual memories. Others will blow your mind and your perception of being, changing your understanding about yourself and many of the things we each take for granted.

My name is Charles Paul Curcio. And even though you may not know me personally, I am your brother and your friend. I have significant things to share with you, things that may change your life, your perspective, and your perception of who you are, what you are, and what you're doing here. This is a true story, my story, the story of how one of seven children from a poor Italian-American family lived and experienced the American Dream, and then found something of far greater value. I have been directed to tell my story, which is really our story, the story of all of God's children who participate in this grand cosmic drama known as the Human Idea. The fact that you are reading this book is no accident, for it's God speaking to you through me.

As you read and receive these words, these pages, these truths, I ask one thing of you, and that is that you exercise discernment. Not just for what you read here, but also about all those so-called truths we have all taken for granted. At no time in human history has the need for discernment been greater. The mind is a wonderful thing, a great gift of the Divine that enables us to think, to reason, to make choices, and most importantly, to know ourselves. But the mind can often confuse and mislead us, and is subject to the pitfalls of the emotions and the desires. The heart is always true. You can tell the truth to someone a million times, yet the truth remains elusive. But just let them feel it once, and they will be a believer. The truth is in the feeling.

As you read what I have to say, breathe in the words, the ideas, the concepts. Feel them within your heart and then allow your heart to decide if they "feel" right or not. If it feels right then embrace it. Don't accept traditional thinking, what you've been told, what you've formerly accepted as true, unless it feels right to you. Make your own choices. Make them from your heart. If you do, you will know the truth, and you will begin to discover a whole new aspect of yourself that will lead you to a greater understanding of life and being. But I caution you as well. Once you receive what I have to share with you, and embrace the things I have to tell you, your life will never be the same. Once you know the truth you can't go back. I'm betting you won't want to anyway. So if you would continue, set your intentions. Set your intentions to know what you need to know and to do what you need to do. Set your intention to know who and what you really are, and why you're really here on earth. For if you do, I promise that you're going to be surprised. Really surprised.

CHAPTER TWO

I Live the American Dream

Let me begin my story by telling you a little about myself. I was born in Philadelphia on July 23, 1948, the first day of Leo, on a day the moon was full. Perhaps I came into this world to share my light, or maybe to discover it myself. Perhaps both. My parents were the children of Italian immigrants, and our family was poor. I was the eldest son and the second oldest in our family of four girls and three boys. My father abandoned our family when I was fourteen, and my mom struggled and raised seven children by herself, working two jobs as a waitress. What a great and simple woman my mom. A million cups of coffee and ten million smiles and kind words crossing her counter and her tables. I never realized what a high spiritual being she was until after she crossed over. She made people smile, and laugh, and feel good about themselves. The greatest ones are usually the most humble.

At the age of nine I took an interest in God. My grandmother Rosa Eizzo was my mentor. She introduced me to St. Mary's Catholic Church, Italian funerals in the old neighborhood, home cooking, and the Philly Steak Sandwich, of which she was the true inventor and originator. She also taught me how to use my hands for healing. Each Saturday, after working all day making steaks and hoagies in my dad's steak shop, I would go to see my grandmother. In her broken English she would ask me to put my hands on her knees and her ankles, wherever she felt pain. Occasionally she would take me around to her friends in the neighborhood and ask me to do the same for them. Back then, I never really understood why she had me do this, or why she or others felt happiness and relief from it, and I lost all memory of it until 40 years later.

At seventeen I quit high school and joined the Marines. After a stint at the Norfolk Naval Base and the Marine Barracks there, I learned Morse Code, which I never used, and by the end of that year, in December of 1966, I found myself humping a radio with an Engineer Battalion in Vietnam. In Vietnam I saw everything there is to see without ever really being embroiled in it. The first person I saw killed was walking 10 feet in front of me as a single shot from a sniper took him down. By the time I crawled to him, calling for a medevac on my radio as I did, he was gone. He had 12 days left in country. Stories like this were common in the 'Nam'. But I myself was always fortunate, in fact blessed, even though I didn't know or realize it. On one occasion, the same day I rotated back out of the field for R and R (5 days of rest and relaxation in Bangkok in this case), my replacement and our unit were overrun that night. Another time, our entire battalion rode a truck convoy through the ancient imperial city of Hue on the same day as the Tet Offensive. That night, all hell broke loose as we passively took up our positions guarding a modestly-used airfield in Quang Tri City 40 miles away.

In Vietnam I was always one step and one day away from trouble. And it felt like to me that there was always some force getting in between myself and danger, between me and the 'action' so to speak, and I was both puzzled and annoyed by it. In Vietnam, I also began to believe that God did not exist and on occasion would say so. After all, I believed and followed the Judeo-Christian tenet of an all-knowing, all-loving, all-merciful and all-powerful God. But I could not reconcile within my heart or my mind the fact that a God who possessed these fine attributes and this much power would create or allow a world in which so much suffering occurred.

After Vietnam, I came back to discover that the world had changed, a lot! Instead of throwing punches, the friends I knew were now throwing peace signs. The consciousness had expanded and the hippie was born. Actually there were far more "hip" people than there were true hippies. Many people were what they called "weekend hippies". I was one of those. But it was cool and so were the times and the people then. We cared about each other and the energy of love blossomed and expanded. We even stopped the war and changed the world. The Baby Boomers came in after that dark night they called World War II and made a difference. After all, wasn't that the plan?

Soon I was married, and had a young son. I managed a two year degree from Montgomery County Community College, alternating between day and night school, and I graduated

Summa Cum Laude. I worked full time for a drug maker then, William H. Rorer, the makers of Maalox, and I was a member of the Teamsters Union. I also fancied myself a social reformer. I embraced progressive and socialistic ideals such as redistribution of wealth, workers owning the means of production, and social justice. It wasn't until I was on a march with the Vietnam Veterans Against the War that I had what I call my "watershed moment". As we passed the Federal Courthouse in Philadelphia, many of my brothers took aim and fired their plastic M16's at the courthouse building. I could understand their frustration, the feeling of being used and then discarded by our country, and the disdain many people showed towards us. But at that moment I realized the folly in this type of behavior. I mean after all, the country may not have been perfect, but America is a beacon of light and freedom shining in the world, the best there's ever been. I realized right then and there that if I took care of myself and my family, and everyone else did the same, things would work out just fine and the world would be a much better place. So in that moment I made a pivot, and I decided to do just that, to take care of myself and my own. This was my first spiritual awakening, although at the time I didn't know it.

I worked for Rorer for a few years and I attended Montgomery County Community College at the same time. After graduation, I moved my family to Palm Beach Gardens, Florida where I started my company, Tire Kingdom, 'on a shoestring and a dime', as my Mom used to say, and found my success in the unlikeliest of vocations. Starting with $500 and no real business or tire experience, I opened Tire Kingdom in the Farmers Market in West Palm Beach, the so-called Miracle Aisle. I soon learned why they called the market this, because it was a miracle if anyone ever found their way to the back of the place where I was obscurely located in the nearly quarter-mile long structure.

Initially I struggled, and I would go days at a time without making a sale, and even when I made one, I made only a couple of dollars at best. The cash and carry sales of tires wasn't working, so I borrowed five hundred dollars and bought some used tire mounting equipment and started mounting tires in the parking lot, something I had to learn how to do. Business improved somewhat but I was barely getting by. But I soon discovered the effectiveness of advertising, the first time in a print advertisement sponsored by the Farmer's Market. But my big breakthrough and my claim to fame would be through TV advertising. So I began doing my own commercials and running them on late night TV, the only times I could afford. Since I couldn't afford a professional spokesperson either, I became the pitchman for my company, something I did for 24 years. And although we first played to a very limited audience, the spots were effective because we always made offbeat commercials that people remembered, and we sold tires for less.

I faced a number of challenges in the tire business which I overcame and was soon the largest tire dealer in Florida, and also ranked number four in the country among independents. I loved Tire Kingdom and the people who worked there. It was my creation and my baby. And we were family. The thing of which I was most proud was the opportunities we gave to ordinary people to learn, to develop, to advance, and to earn. Thousands of people grew and thrived in our ranks, many of who moved on to bigger and better opportunities in other fields. Tire Kingdom was the springboard to their success. We didn't care as much about their education or qualifications as we did about their work ethic, common sense, and willingness to learn and work hard. At TK we all worked hard. Our doors were open to everyone who was willing to do the same.

In 1989 I sold the company to French tire maker Michelin, although I continued at the helm and was given the independence to run the company as I saw fit. Under Michelin I doubled the size of the company, and I earned another big payday. Then Michelin decided to sell the company to raise capital, as they were in difficult financial shape. Three years later, I partnered with Goldman Sachs and another Wall Street firm, and we bought back the company. I signed a four year employment agreement with my new partners and continued running Tire Kingdom as I always had.

In my life and in my business career I had achieved the American Dream. Starting with virtually nothing, I now had everything the world says you should have – money, success, fame, a loving wife and beautiful children, an oceanfront mansion, luxury cars, the toys, all that one could claim. But deep inside of me there was something missing. On October 1st, 1995 something incredible happened, something that would change my life forever.

CHAPTER THREE

The New Day
I speak with God

One summer morning as I was driving to work, I was flipping through the channels on the radio, and I heard an interview with a woman who was claiming sexual discrimination by her company. When I realized she was talking about us, I nearly ran my car off the road. Why would she do and say such things? I was in shock. Two months earlier, after much encouragement and convincing by us, she agreed to take a promotion as one of store managers. We were expanding rapidly, and we needed store managers. But she wasn't ready, and she requested that we place her back in her previous job as an assistant manager, which we did. Apparently her brother had convinced her that if she made the claim, we would pay her off just to make her go away. She subsequently got involved with a woman's group who went on the attack. Each time they invented a new and bogus claim we would respond and refute it. And then they would invent another. What followed was an incredible public relations campaign against us which culminated in a media circus covered by every major media outlet in South Florida. And in the end we stood together and won the PR battle. But I was left feeling attacked and violated, and alone.

The next day was Sunday October 1, 1995. I got up early in the morning and was feeling really down. But I followed my normal Sunday routine which was to drive around my property in a golf cart and experience and appreciate the beautiful trees, flowers, birds, fish, and other wildlife there. I lived on Jupiter Island, one of the most beautiful and captivating places on the planet. Thanks to my business success, I owned ten acres which stretched from the Atlantic Ocean to the Indian River. Every type of fauna and flora in the Atlantic Ecosystem existed and flourished in my little piece of paradise. But where I normally took great pleasure just being in nature, on this day I was feeling very low and depressed. Instead of driving the golf cart with the roof, I decided to take the one without a roof, the one typically used by my property caretaker, something I had never done before.

The peace, the joy, the enthusiasm for nature that I normally felt on these Sundays was missing today. I felt just awful. I just couldn't shake the feeling. And even though I followed my normal routine; no matter how beautiful my surroundings, I was still upset. I made my way down to the Indian River, the Intracoastal Waterway, and I startled a blue heron that was nesting on my dock. Schools of mullet were migrating south, and the water was constantly exploding from the feeding activity of the snook, jacks, and barracuda, and the mullet that were skyrocketing to avoid these attacks. Normally, I would have been overjoyed at seeing these things, and would have gathered my fishing rod and bait casting net and joined in the action. But today I was too depressed. So I got back into my cart and followed the winding cart path back to my house.

The path itself ran under a series of magnificent banyan trees, many of which were over a hundred years old. On my ride back, I suddenly stopped under one of these banyans and looked up. I had no idea why I did this. At that moment I remembered reading once that the Buddha received enlightenment under a banyan tree. Now I didn't know much if anything about Buddha, and I wondered why the thought of him would come into my mind at that moment. I flashed back to the events of the previous day and weeks. I could feel my emotions as I was overcome by them, and the feelings of outrage, anger, shame, and self-pity that I felt all at the same time. I looked up again, and I cried out, "Why God, why does this crap always happen to me?"

Suddenly, at that moment I was jolted by a surge of energy. My body shuddered and I almost fell out of the cart. It was as if I was hit by lightning as I was overcome with the energy that now surged through me. And then, out of my mouth in a voice that wasn't mine came the answer to my question: "Because you have purpose Charles". "What, who was that?" I stammered. And then the voice spoke again, "You know", came the reply. Nothing is stranger than to hear words spontaneously coming out of one's own mouth in a voice that isn't yours. But the voice was right, I did know who it was, although maybe deep down I didn't want to. "God, is that you?" I asked sheepishly. And God answered, "Yes my son. I came to ask you if you're ready".

Confused and dazed I replied, "Ready, ready for what?" And then he answered, "Ready to serve me". I began to weep. "Father, I've really been struggling", I sobbed. And He said to me, "I know you have Charles, that's why I've come." All at once I could feel His majesty and His humility. It was if I could see and experience the many facets of God all at the same time. And I realized this was all much bigger than me.

Waves of understanding and an incredible love washed over me. And then it hit me. I was talking with God! My sadness was quickly replaced by jubilation and excitement, and also fear. "Oh my God, you're really here! You really are. You really exist. You really love me." And in that moment I knew so much. I knew everything, and I knew nothing. In a flash I understood that our earth lives are like a drama, a grand cosmic play in which we all participate. We live the ultimate theatre, in which we take on different roles at different times in our existence, spiritual beings all, trying to be human, endeavoring to become whole. We come to experience the physical world, assuming many faces and many personalities in many times and many places, going where the action is, trying to perfect our being, to discharge our karma, and always seeking to bring our Higher Selves, our Spirit, fully into matter. 'It's a game' was the phrase I heard in my mind. Being a big sports fan I realized this was something we had in common. I said aloud and to myself, "It's a game. God likes games!"

My emotions began to alternate between fear and excitement. I began laughing hysterically with excitement, and in the next moment I was trembling in fear. I started questioning. I started thinking of and asking questions, and He gave me every answer. Just as fast as I could ask or think of a question, the answer would come out of my mouth instantly or I received it telepathically. For the next hour or so, I don't know exactly how long, it was like this. God would speak and I would listen. I would ask and God would answer. I knew the love of God as well as the fear of Him firsthand. And then He hit me with it, the reason He had come. "Charles, your earth life is far more than you believe it to be, and you have come here with a purpose, My purpose. And now I am asking you if you are willing, and ready to fulfill it." I couldn't imagine what this purpose was or what God could possibly want from me. And even though my role in any of this was unclear to me, I became afraid and I began to feel my own unworthiness, and I said, "Father, who am I, that you would want me? There must be others who are better qualified, more suitable, more worthy than I to do your work." And God replied simply, "It's you that I'm asking Charles." And I said, "But you know me Lord and you know my faults. Why would you want me? You can have anyone you want. Please, find someone who is better, someone more suitable and capable." And again I asked, "Why would you want me?" And God said, "Because you are the one I have chosen. Will you do what I am asking?"

I had no retort now, nothing to say. For the first time in my life I was speechless. When God asks you for something, it's pretty hard to say no. Finally I said, "God, I don't know why you've come to me or even if any of this is real. But if you're sure it's me that you want, then I will do whatever you ask of me. Thy will be done." And then He said, "Thank you my son. I love you". And I replied, "I love you too God."

And then, sensing he was about to leave and realizing I had no clue what he wanted, I cried out, "But God, What is it that you want me to do?" And then He answered, "You are to learn about me Charles, and about you, and then teach others who they are too. You will know and learn much. You will know everything when it is time." And then it ended, just as suddenly as it had begun.

No one was more surprised or confused by these events than I was. I was in a daze. One moment I was feeling sorry for myself, and in the next I was engaged in a conversation with God. "Did that really just happen?" I asked myself. I wasn't sure. I wasn't sure of anything. The cares, the worries, the concerns I had been feeling just a little while earlier were just a faded memory. They were now meaningless and of no account. Instead they were replaced with feelings of jubilation and excitement. I was so alive, so energized, so high, and so confused. Again I asked myself if what had just happened was real. I wasn't sure. What I was sure of is that something incredible had just occurred and all of a sudden I got excited. God had spoken to me and he wants me to work for him! Holy Cow! In my excitement I started to run up to my house to tell my wife. I was feeling giddy as I said to myself, "Man I can't wait to tell Jill and the boys." And then it hit me, and I stopped dead in my tracks and said to myself, "Oh my God, so this is what it's like to go crazy!"

I felt the energy of fear wash over me. My body began to shake, and I began to doubt. "What if that didn't really happen? What if I'm just having a nervous breakdown?" I then started to rationalize things as I told myself, "Well you have been under a lot of pressure and stress lately, and besides, why would God want anything to do with you?" And then I started to reason back and forth with myself, asking and answering my own questions. Finally, I thought I'd finally lost my mind. I was in total shock. I didn't want to believe what just happened, and I didn't want to believe it didn't. But one thing was sure, something did indeed happen, and I knew in my heart that it just wasn't going to go away.

I stopped running towards the house and turned around and walked back to the golf cart. I got in and drove back up to the basketball court. I took a couple of shots, but my heart just wasn't in it, and I went inside the house. I saw my wife Jill there and she recognized that something was troubling me. She asked me what the matter was. I said, "Oh nothing, I'm still a little bummed out from yesterday." She said, "Don't worry. That's all over now and you'll deal with it just like you always do." I wanted to tell her what really happened, but I didn't know what to say. So I said nothing. On the TV, the football game was just starting. I was an avid Miami Dolphins fan, and I lived or died each week on the outcome of their games. On this afternoon however, I tried to watch it but I just couldn't get into it. This had never happened to me before. I piddled around the house for a while, but couldn't get settled into anything. The events of the morning as well as my own mental and emotional state weighed heavily upon me. So I decided to go over to the beach and feel the ocean, and the sun, and the wind upon my face. The sea always fortified and reju- venated me whenever I needed it.

Later that afternoon, I crossed South Beach Road and

walked onto the dune crossover which adjoined the deck of my little beach house. I often came here when I had something to ponder. Never had I had so much to think about as I did this day. I sat in one of the gliders on the deck that surrounded the house, and I began to rock myself gently. The sun was bright and the sky was a striking blue with just a hint of clouds. The ocean was a vivid turquoise, the color one might associate with a Caribbean island, but which was always in evidence here as well. A gentle breeze blew upon my face and I thought how beautiful this place and this day really were. I took a deep breath, looked up, and I asked, "God, was that really you?"

Instantly I felt the waves of energy move into me once more. Only this time I was being impulsed by many sources all at once. I began to agonize within, and I could hear myself whining in my reaction to the energy, as I heard the words, "Remember who you are". Then I started to receive impulses and images of a dramatically changing world, thoughts of Nostradamus, of Plato and Aristotle, of the Middle East, of armies of soldiers preparing and forming up for the looming battles of the darkness and the light. I could see them on multiple levels. I saw tank and infantry formations in the physical world, cavalry formations in the Astral World, and winged warriors in the higher planes. I heard other words too, and sounds and speech and language I didn't recognize. Then I saw armies of modern day soldiers and tanks moving through the sands of the desert kicking up great clouds of dust, along with charioteers and cavalry, and archers and various life forms I didn't recognize. And then the visions became more complex and more intense and I had a hard time even following them. There were just so many images and symbols, and so much activity and light moving so fast across my field of vision that my mind couldn't comprehend any of it. Then I saw the sky open up, and a great blinding light emanating and streaming down through the opening. I tried to close my eyes, but they were already closed. And I heard His voice once again: "Charles, will you follow me in the task that you have chosen?" Again I resisted.

"Father, I don't understand anything. I don't understand what you want and I don't remember choosing anything. I'm not even sure that any of this is real. Surely there are so many you can pick from. Maybe a priest or a holy man, someone who is better suited than I." And calmly God replied, "Dear one, if there were another appointed I would have come to them. But you are the one I'm asking." And I said, "Lord you know I love you. And I would do anything you ask. But surely there are those who are more deserving, more capable than me." And then I realized why I was resisting. I was afraid I wasn't up to the task and would surely let Him down, something I then felt I had done before. And He knew. And He said simply, "You can do it Charles." And I felt the truth of it. So I said, "Father, I will do as you ask. Thy will be done." And God replied, "I love you son", and then He was gone. And for the second time in the same day it happened and then ended.

As I was driving the cart back over to the main house, there on my front lawn was a rabbit, about ten feet from me. According to my caretaker, here on Jupiter Island we had a lot of rabbits, but they fed mostly at night, and I don't think I ever saw one here. But on this day there was one in plain view that wasn't even startled by my presence or the mechanical noise of the golf cart. I had always loved rabbits since I was little boy. I would often watch them and try to locate their nests, just so I could keep tabs on the young ones as they grew and developed. I drove by the rabbit, who didn't budge, and drove out of sight when I realized that this was a sign. I determined that if that rabbit were still there when I went back, then it meant that all of what had happened this day was true. Sure enough, when I want back, there was my little friend. He stopped munching the grass and then looked straight into my eyes for what seemed an eternity, and then he resumed his munching. Only when I drove away did he finally go.

When I reached the house, my oldest son Jason and his girlfriend Christi were sitting on the front steps. I was so excited now and so exuberant and so sure about what had happened that I just had to tell someone. I said to them, "You won't believe this but I was just talking to God." They both looked at me kind of puzzled and surprised as I began to them the story. Jason rolled his eyes and Christi's got wider as I continued, "It happened twice today, earlier this morning and again this afternoon." Jason said to me, "Huh, what do you mean Dad?" And I said, "Son, I mean exactly what I said." I went on to tell them a little of what had happened and that I felt it would change my life. When I finished, they were both very quiet, as they had taken it all in and they believed what I said. "That's really cool Dad", said Jason, and Christi said, "Wow Mr. C, that's really neat". I told them, "Yeah, thanks. It really is special. I think I'll go in now and tell your mom." Inside I went to find Jill who was in the kitchen.

I said to her, "Honey you won't believe this but I just had a talk with God. That's what I wanted to tell you this morning, but I just didn't know how." She looked at me, paused, and then she smiled. She placed her hand on my forehead as if she was checking to see if I had a fever, and then she said, "Honey are you ok? I think you're under a lot of stress". And I said, "No honey, really. God spoke to me twice today and he wants me to do something for Him." To this she replied, "Why don't you go lie down and watch the game or a movie or something. Everything's going to be okay." It was clear that Jill didn't believe me, and she was attributing my strange behavior to stress. I didn't feel like trying to convince her otherwise, and I decided then that I wasn't going to tell this story to too many people.

Later that evening, I was sitting on my back porch at sunset when He came to me once more. Only this time all of my anxiety and all of my resistance was gone. I already knew why He had come. When I felt His Presence, I asked Him, "Father, are you sure that it's me that you want? Isn't there someone else, someone better than I?" And God responded, "Charles, you are the one I am asking". And I answered, "I love you God, and I will do whatever you want me to do. Thy will be done." After a pause, a pause I feel He allowed me so that I could be sure of my choice, He said, "Thank you Charles. Know that I am with you always". And I said, "Thank you God, thank you for everything." And then it was all over. At that instant I remembered that the Christ had asked for his cup to be taken away from him three times too, just as I had done this day. And I knew in that moment that my life would never be the same again.

CHAPTER FOUR

I Begin my Spiritual Healing and Training

After that Sunday morning, events in my life began to sequence and to change, often moving at lightning speed. I began doing past life regression at the Brian Weiss Institute in South Miami, and from my past lives I gained a great deal of understanding about my current life and circumstances. Many of the same players and people (members of my soul group) were back in my current life, and I was being given new opportunities from which to learn, and to make better choices. I also gained a great deal of understanding about why I felt the way I did. By connecting with a previous self in a past life and experiencing the events of that lifetime, I was able to see how the faulty thoughts, unbalanced emotions, or past life events affected my current life. I also discovered that we all have a number of Spirit Guides that assist us in our journey. Most stay with us until an aspect or evolutionary stage of our growth is completed, and then they move on and are replaced with others who take us to the next level. I had many guides prior to my arrival at Delphi. One of them was an old friend named Augustus with whom I shared many lifetimes, and who accompanied me on a number of my past life regressions. Augustus liked to wear the hat or headdress of the time period where we travelled. What a character. Each time when I would go to another lifetime he was there waiting for me, wearing the headdress of the period. He was equally comfortable in an ancient Egyptian Nemes Headdress as he was in a cowboy hat. I learned many things about myself and about existence in these past life experiences. And most significantly, I began to learn about the true meaning of love.

Although Past Life Regression opened my eyes (all three of them), it was only the beginning of my journey. Through my past lives, I learned and experienced so much, even experiencing my own death physically and the air rushing out of my collapsing lungs, as well as my spirit leaving my body. And yet death was nothing to fear. It was simply a vibrational change, a transition to our natural spiritual state, and new opportunities to learn, to live, and to express ourselves on earth once again. The fact is we're all eternal beings without beginning or end. What does one do with eternity, and an unlimited Source of energy we call God? As participants in the Grand Divine Plan, the Human Idea, we use it to experience the physical world, this beautiful planet of ours and it's many wonders. We also use it to balance and discharge our Karma, the Law of Cause and Effect, to make better choices, and to make right those things we haven't done so well in the past. In our journey, we get as many chances, as many lifetimes as we need to get it right. This is why we continuously reincarnate. In addition to experiencing the world and balancing our Karma, the most important reason for living is to prepare ourselves and our body temple for the indwelling of our Higher Selves, so that God can be fully present and express Himself on Earth through us. More about that later.

I have learned so many things after stepping on the spiritual path. One of the most significant is that people come into our lives for a purpose. And when that purpose is completed they move on to their next experience, their next lesson, and their next episode, as do we all. These life events and circumstances are planned by us on a soul level with a lot of help from our spiritual friends, and then acted out in the physical world. Many a wise sage has said that the old must depart before the new can come in. I didn't understand then, to where or what this was all leading. But I did know what I wanted, and that was to walk in the light each day, one step at a time, with my head held high, and discover more about my being, my purpose, and about who I really am. My newfound path was mysterious, exciting, uncertain, and compelling, all at the same time. And I was committed to it, no matter where it may lead me. After the Past Life Regression sessions, I felt there was much more for me to do, to learn, and to experience. And magically, I could feel the Universe working behind the scenes, and my new spiritual life was accelerating quickly, as it does for all who make the connection and the commitment. The people, places, circumstances, and events necessary to my spiritual awakening began to occur, in exactly the right order and in exactly the right time, place, and sequence. My life began to take on a whole new meaning and direction. Things were changing rapidly. It was as if I had moved into an energy current, and this current was carrying me downstream towards a destination and a place where I had never traveled before. And so I trusted and went with the flow. It happens that way in Spirit. One day you'll find that out for yourself.

In early 1996, my son Jason called me at work to say hello and to let me know about a new age bookstore that had recently opened in Juno Beach in a location that was on my way home from work. Jason said, "Dad I know you're into that stuff and I thought you'd like to know about it". Jason was right. I was into that 'stuff'. I had begun meditating twice daily and connecting with the world of Sprit. Spiritual beings, information, events, and episodes started to unfold rapidly in my life, as if I was learning something urgent and important, without a moment to spare. Each step was leading to the next.

The next day I opened the telephone to look for the phone number and address and I found two listings for Awakenings. One listing was the bookstore itself, and the other was a listing that said: *Awakenings – Spiritual classes, Aura Photography, and more*. Since this location was only a short distance from my office, I decided to check it out over lunch. When I arrived at the address listed in the phone book, I didn't find the expected Awakenings. Instead the address was that of a certified public accountant's office. When I inquired about Awakenings, the gentlemen told me that I had come to the right place but that his aura camera was broken. Sensing my disappointment, he asked me about myself, and what was going on with me. I told him about much of what had been happening in my life, and he told me he understood what I was saying. Well, this was refreshing. He said that when he had entered upon the spiritual path, he too was having difficulty finding his way, and he recommended I go to see a spiritual counselor and healer in Boca Raton. Her name was Dianne Rosenthal. He gave me her business card and said he would call her to let her know about me. I thanked him and left. That afternoon I called Diane and scheduled an appointment to see her.

Diane worked out of her home in West Boca Raton. When I arrived there and knocked on the door, she was there to greet me. The smell of incense permeated the house and Diane was dressed in flowing white robes. With her long curly red hair and dress, she looked like some kind of ancient priestess from another time and place. Anyone who saw her and the array of crystals, art, and unusual objects she had in her therapy room might have concluded how weird it all seemed. But I felt very comfortable here, as if everything was all very familiar. Even when she used phrases like calling upon the Shekinah (the Hebrew name for the Holy Spirit or Divine Mother aspect of the Godhead) and Yahweh (pronounced Yah-Vey, the Hebrew name for God the Father), I felt so very comfortable, as if I had heard and known these names before.

In her healing work, Diane used a combination of visualization, regression, and spiritual psychotherapy. In our first meditation together, she had me visualize a great hallway with a series of large pillars lining the hall. She asked me how many pillars I saw, and I told her seventeen, which was weird, because the pillars were evenly paired. Behind each pillar was a spirit guide. She told me that each would reveal themselves over time, when I was ready. The first of these new guides was an extremely tall and slender female from the star system Sirius, who had now come to help me develop my sensitivity and feminine energy. She was quite magical, beautiful, and you could just feel the love energy emanating from her. She was also about twelve feet tall. Just being in her vibration was enough to affect mine. Over the next few months, new guides would come in, and the older ones would depart when their work was finished. Even my friend Augustus started to fade and ultimately said goodbye, making way for the new to come through.

Each of us in life possesses a complement of spiritual guides and teachers who are here to aid and assist us on our spiritual path. They are assigned exclusively to us, until their work with us is done. Generally, each of us has at least one pair of guides, a male and a female. Sometimes these guides are androgynous, neither male nor female but possessing the qualities of both. This condition, by the way is wholeness, the combination of male and female energies which each human being possesses, regardless of gender. Your guides are here to help you in every aspect of your life. They have sometimes been referred to as angels, which many of them are. Others might be former friends and loved ones working from the other side, or masters who have perfected human existence like a saint or sage, or an archangelic presence. Each has come to give you what you need. The challenge for human beings is to know they do indeed exist and then to open up to working with them. And of course, one must ask, ask for help. This is a universal law: you must ask for what you want.

If you are skeptical, then I invite you to try the following. Find yourself a quiet comfortable place and close your eyes. Then begin to breathe naturally, in through the nose and out through the mouth. Just let yourself breathe naturally and find the rhythm of your breath, just like the ocean surf. As the surf rolls out you breathe in, and as the surf comes to shore you breathe out. Between each inhale and each exhale there is a short natural pause. If you breathe like this for a few minutes you will feel yourself relax and your consciousness shift. Just let yourself go. Then when you are relaxed, silently call upon your guides and let them know you are ready to work with them. Ask them to reveal themselves to you and they will. Ask them to help you with some life event with which you are having difficulty. You may feel their love energy. You may even feel them touching your head or your hand or your heart. They may also reveal themselves in a way you don't expect such as in something you read or see or hear. As you work with them you will even begin to communicate with them telepathically. Earnestly invite your guides to work with you and you will get results.

For the next few months I worked with Diane to identify, and then to heal and clear those lower energies of fear, anger, shame, and many others, archetypal energies that affect each of us. I saw her weekly and I started to understand more about myself and who I was. At a soul level, I asked all those I had hurt to forgive me, and I forgave all those who had harmed me. Forgiving others is just as important as being forgiven. For to continue to harbor resentment against someone who has hurt you, only hurts yourself in the end, and blocks your ability to receive God's Grace.

The laws of energy are basic and fundamental. The Law of Attraction, for instance, states that "like attracts like". If you are fearful, then you attract fear or events in your life that create fear. Loving thoughts and feelings attract love and higher experiences. An unwillingness to forgive others preempts you from receiving forgiveness, for what you are resonating, the vibration that you are putting out, is the opposite of what you want to attract to yourself.

Each of us begins our human journey as perfect or whole, a true reflection of our God, of which we are a part. If God were an ocean and you were to dip a cup into this ocean, what would then be in the cup is you, your Divine Person, your Higher Self. You are not something separate, not a creation, but a piece of God Himself. You are not 'made' or 'created' by God, no more than you are made in America or made in China. Rather, you are expressed by God from within Himself. The result of this expression and projection is the Higher Self, your Permanent Personality. The Higher Self then projects a part of itself into earth as a temporary personality, you, in which to express itself and experience human life and physical existence.

When are journey began, our first and fundamental purpose was to create a sense of self, an ego, the development and awareness of our own individual person. Prior to the process of Creation, or more appropriately described, manifestation, the only being that possessed a sense of self or individual awareness was God. Once we enter into the Divine Plan and separate from God, each of us is tasked to discover ourselves. In order to develop a sense of self, one must first become self-ish. And the condition of selfishness is a necessary part of the plan of human spiritual evolution. Once the lower self or ego is established, then the life task becomes to evolve that self from the state of taking to giving, from selfishness to selflessness, from conditional love to unconditional love. The evolution of self progresses from the lower self to the Higher Self or God Self, which is our true nature. This takes many, many lifetimes to accomplish and is why reincarnation and the cycle of death and rebirth is a necessary part of the Divine Plan.

If one were to go deep within one's own heart, and strip away all that keeps us separate from God, what we would find there was God Himself. The separation we feel is an illusion. There is only One, and we are all a part of the whole, expressing ourselves individually. For you see, God experiences himself through us, His manifestation. Just like our Father, we have the same abilities and attributes, the most fundamental of which is the ability of creation. Each of us is the creator of our lives. Each time we have a thought, particularly if that thought is energized by desire, we create a conscious, active, living thoughtform with only one purpose, to fulfill the wish of its creator. Throughout our many incarnations, each time we have done something ungodly, each time we feel, think, or express our lower emotions, thoughts, or intentions, we create or attract lower energies into our energy fields that block and prevent us from expressing our true nature. It is as if we were inside a clear bubble of glass, and with every selfish or negative thought, act, or emotion, we throw mud against the glass. Soon the bubble is completely covered and we are surrounded by the darkness we have created, and light no longer shines in or out.

As a result of these activities we have also created Karma. Karma is the Divine Law of Balance, of Cause and Effect. If we cause something to happen, the effect is that we are responsible for everything we cause or do. If we harm another, then the effect is that we are responsible for what we have done. Karma can be satisfied through asking for and receiving forgiveness from the person we have hurt, by gaining the understanding of the harm we have caused others, by experiencing the same hurt ourselves, sometimes at the hand of the offended person, or by asking for and receiving God's grace. But usually we will have to uncover, experience, understand, and process these lower energies in order to heal them. The Ten Commandments were not rules of behavior, but rather, Karmic Laws. The Old Testament proscription, "An eye for an eye, and a tooth for a tooth", was a statement of Karmic Law and effect, and not an authorization for revenge. Today with the evolution of the planet and the greater energies of love and light being shined upon it, and the activities of all aware people to heal and grow, energetically leaving a map or path for others to follow, it is possible now, more than ever before, to heal yourself and to discover who and what you really are.

Throughout my life, my children have been a constant source of pleasure for me. My family was the reason I worked so hard to give them all that I thought was important and desirable in life. My three boys were all born on the eighteenth day of the month, Timmy on January eighteenth, Michael on February eighteenth, and Jason on May eighteenth. I haven't yet figured out why this is important, but I'm sure one day I will understand the significance. In January of 1996, Timmy, the youngest of my children, had his sixteenth birthday. I was very excited about this and I bought him a brand new BMW M3 for his first car. Even though today's M3's are far more sophisticated vehicles, nevertheless it was really cool, particularly for a young man's first car. It was what Timmy had wanted, and it was a surprise to him. We had it parked in the driveway with a big red bow upon it on the morning of his birthday. Since it was a school day, we all got up early to hold a little morning celebration beforehand. It was a beautiful morning and we were all very happy, particularly Timmy. It was really great to watch him drive away in his new car. After Tim had gone, I said goodbye to Jill and headed out the front door to go to work. As I walked through the foyer, suddenly I was overcome with fear. My knees buckled, and all of a sudden it hit me as I involuntarily exclaimed, "Oh my God, my baby's all grown up. What in the world am I gonna do now?" I realized that raising my children had been my purpose in life, the reason I worked so hard, the reason I never quit. And now, that purpose no longer seemed valid.

CHAPTER FIVE

Things That Should Have Been Strange Really Weren't

In February I was invited to a birthday party thrown by my friend John Boswell for his mother-in-law on a Saturday afternoon. It was a small but splendid affair attended by a caterer and a dozen guests. For entertainment, John had hired a psychic reader to do readings for each of the people who had come. I was the last one to see the reader, and I was preceded by my wife Jill. Jill had a kind of secretive smile on her face when she came out, and to this day I don't know what the psychic told her, as Jill would never tell me. I do know what the psychic said to me. When I entered the room, the reader whose name was Gloria said hello and invited me to sit down. The first thing she told me was, "Well, it looks like you're going to divorce your wife and move to the mountains." I was stunned and speechless. I stammered and tried to compose myself, but all I could say was, "What?" Gloria then repeated what she had said. The last thing I intended to do was to divorce Jill or to break up my family. I said, "That's it? That's what you have to say to me?" I couldn't believe what I was hearing, and I was shocked that she would say it in such a direct way. She smiled, consulted her Tarot deck again, and said, "What I have told you is right. I don't typically do these kinds of affairs, but when I do, I usually have something important to say to one of the people there. Today I believe that person is you." Even though I felt the truth of what she said inside, I asked, "Are you sure? Are you sure there isn't some kind of mistake?" When she replied that she was certain, I then asked, "Do you know when?" And she told me, "Yes, within two years." And when I asked her which mountains, she consulted her astrological star charts, and after some consideration she said, "Looks like the Blue Ridge Mountains." Bewildered, I thanked her and I left.

Well I certainly had a lot to ponder. Just when I thought I was getting comfortable, I realized that I wasn't. In Spirit, sometimes the obvious things are not so obvious. Sometimes the things you think are inappropriate or wrong, are the catalysts for change, and are consistent with the plans and the agreement of all those involved, even if they only know it at a soul level. Until you tap into the power of your spirit and make the conscious connection, you may never know the truth, the truth of who you are, the reasons certain things happen in your life, and what your life plan actually is. Unless you make the connection with your Higher Self, typically through meditation and spiritual practice, you cannot receive the Divine Gifts that are you birthright.

What was going on in my life? The only thing of which I was certain was that my life was changing. Change. The one and only constant in life. I decided that if Spirit did indeed have a plan for me, and if that plan meant I had to leave my wife and family for places and things unknown, then that's what I would do, painful as it might be. I decided to let things unfold in their natural order, and not to worry about it. I knew I was in good hands, the best there are, and I would let God decide my fate. After all, I had made the commitment to God Himself. It was this commitment and this knowing that would carry me through, no matter what the circumstances and how difficult they seemed or ultimately would become.

The last Friday evening of each month, Dianne Rosenthal would host a spiritual event at her home for her clients. At each of these events, she would invite a speaker, or a healer, or in the case of the first event I attended, a trance channel. A trance channel is someone whose personality steps aside and allows a spiritual being to incorporate their body in order to speak with those people in attendance. It was all pretty wild, and in some ways it reminded me of the movie Ghost. Only this was real. On this night, the channel was a man from Fort Lauderdale who was said to bring through Metatron, the first of the Archangels manifested by God, whose name in Hebrew is El Shaddai. As I watched the channel prepare and begin to take deep and directed breaths, I saw his countenance change before my eyes. He was still the same person, but he looked different. And when the incorporation seemed complete, out of his mouth came the voice of a woman. This particular spirit had come to prepare the way for Metatron and that's what she told us. Then we all waited as Metatron was first announced and then arrived.

The channel seemed to be having difficulty in allowing Metatron to incorporate his body. But when he finally did, the first thing Metatron did was to apologize about the delay and then he made a joke about how it wasn't easy to get his fifteen foot frame inside this five foot man. Metatron spoke to us about life, about existence and how it works, and about things we could do to heal ourselves and improve our connection with spirit. I have to say that, even though I wasn't sure I was buying into any of this, everything he had to say was intriguing, and many of the truths he revealed were amazing. At the end of the session he asked if there were any of us who wanted to ask him a question, and many did. One woman, who had been unable to get pregnant for years, asked if there was a way she could accomplish it. He advised her to eat an unshelled walnut every day for a month. A month later she became pregnant. After some reluctance on my part, I asked for clarity about my own situation. He said simply, "We ask that you take your time and be sure of what you do". He continued, "Do you understand our meaning in this?" And somehow I did understand and I told him I would. And then he said to the group, ""So that you will know that what I say tonight is from Spirit, each of you will have a significant dream within the next two days." And then he thanked us, told us of Spirit's unwavering love for us, and then he departed.

The next night I had an amazing dream. I was at a big celebration of spiritual beings, all who I knew. Everyone there who was currently incarnate was being honored and celebrated for having made the descent into matter, for the challenges they faced, the progress and sacrifices they were making on the earth plane, and for expanding God's presence in the physical world. Gathered around and loving us were a myriad of wonderful and incredibly beautiful spiritual beings. And each one of us was just as beautiful. In our spiritual form we were just like them, and they were just like us. In the morning I woke up so joyful, so fulfilled, and so happy at the events I had just experienced, that I was in a daze. And I realized that what Metatron had predicted had come true. After trying to return to the dream unsuccessfully, I laid there and wondered if the others in the group had experienced the same thing. And in an instant I knew that each one had experienced something unique, something different, and something that was important and necessary for them. Myself I realized how much each of us is loved and that we're never alone.

Because of my love of astrology, I scheduled an appointment with a well-known astrologer in Hollywood named Barbara Bunch. Although she was booked solid for the next four months, as luck or fate would have it, she had a cancellation within the week, and I was invited to take the appointment. I was born on July 23rd, 1948, the first day of Leo in the astrological charts. Barbara told me that the moon was full on the day of my birth, and that July 23rd is also the day when the star system Sirius is closest to earth. If you are in the Southern Hemisphere on the morning of July 23rd, a small brilliant red ball of light will rise on the horizon two minutes before the sunrise, and only on July 23rd. This ball of light is Sirius, which is really two stars, one rotating around another. Upon reading my chart, Barbara told me that starting towards the end of '95, a number of spiritual events had occurred and would continue to occur in my life, culminating at the end of July and perhaps into early August of that year. She told me that a number of spiritual friends, both incarnate and discarnate, would come into my life, give me a gift or gifts, and then would move out just as quickly as they had come in, and just in time for the next to arrive. She said that it had always been this way with me, that I was never early, but always just on time. Everything she said was consistent with what had happened and was happening to me. After it was over, she asked me if I had any questions. I had none, for I understood everything she said.

In the weeks and months that followed, I was absorbed in and fascinated by Spirit, and was doing all I could or thought I should do to learn and to grow. I was meditating twice daily, attending workshops and channelings, reading intently, and collecting everything I could find that was metaphysical. When I would go into a new age bookstore, books would literally fall off the shelves or fall on my head. I'm not kidding. It was a very exciting time for me, and I was all excited and enthusiastic over God and Spirit. I never dreamed that such things existed, and the pursuit of Spirit became my entire focus. I even lost interest in my work, something I had never even considered before. Weeks after my son Jason had told me about it, I finally paid a visit to the Awakenings Bookstore. It was just after six in the evening when I walked in, and I was the only customer in the place. Behind the counter was a woman who looked up at me the moment I entered. Immediately and without any hesitation she said to me, "You need to go to Delphi". Puzzled, I responded, "Delphi, what is that, like some place in Greece?" I knew nothing about Greek culture, history, or geography, except that I had vaguely heard about Delphi and its famous oracle. And she answered, "No, it's a spiritual school in the mountains of North Georgia. I don't know why I'm saying this, but I feel compelled to tell you. I was a student there some time ago, and I think I may have a brochure in the back of the store. I'll go look." And with that she disappeared into the back room to search for it.

About ten minutes later, the owner, whose name was Karen Walther, reappeared with a tattered one page leaflet which was titled "In Depth Channeling at Delphi University", and gave it to me. I thanked her, bought a couple of the more hard-hitting titles (pun intended), collected all the brochures, fliers, and leaflets she had available in the store, and left. The next day at my office, I placed the Delphi flier as well as all the other things I had collected into the ever-growing metaphysical pile on my desk. After all, I had an increasing number of places to go and things to do, and Delphi was just another possibility. But I did remember that Dianne had told me a month before this, that my path would likely lead me to some type of spiritual school. Later that afternoon, I was reentering my office when I tripped over my phone cord. I extended my arms to break my fall, and I caught myself on the edge of my desk. As I landed, my right hand struck the pile, and all the papers careened off the opposite side of my desk, all save one.

As I watched the stack disappear over the edge, out popped the Delphi flyer to the left, which then spun very slowly three complete times before coming to rest in the center of my desk. It occurred to me how unusual this seemed, and then I did what so many of us do when we experience phenomena or paranormal events. I blew it off and rationalized it away. I picked up the flyer and the other papers and reformed the pile, not giving it another thought. The next morning my administrative assistant Beth walked into my office, mirrored my trip from the previous day, and knocked over the pile too. Only this time I was seated at my desk. And just like before, the Delphi brochure popped out, spun three times interminably slowly, and landed in the middle of my desk. I asked Beth if she had seen what had just happened, and she said, "Yeah, that was pretty weird". I told her that I thought so too. And with that I instructed her to give Delphi a call, that I wanted to go there. I signed up for the upcoming In-Depth Channeling class they taught there, and I was scheduled to arrive on August ninth, a few months later. I didn't really have any idea what I would learn or experience there, but I was sure that this was a sign from the Universe that was meant for me to follow. After all, Spirit only had to show me twice in dramatic fashion for me to get it.

In April, I attended another of Diane's monthly gatherings. At this one there were a pair of healers, a married couple from India, who were demonstrating the Reiki method of hands-on healing. I thought this demonstration was fascinating. Reiki is a method of energy healing that has its roots in the Far East, particularly Japan. Basically, a Reiki healer will invoke and call upon the universal energies of healing and the help and assistance of all the Reiki Masters who preceded him, both incarnate and discarnate, and then channel these energies through his or her hands and to their clients while touching them. All forms of energy healing where the healer places his hands upon the person seeking healing is called "hands-on healing". Unlike trance channeling though, the healer is fully conscious and is only channeling the healing energies, and not the consciousness of another being. As they channel the energy, the healer's hands often become very hot from the energy that is flowing through them. As the healers were demonstrating their technique, I could actually feel the energy they were channeling, as could many others in the room. Without thinking, I looked at Diane who at that exact moment looked at me, and we both understood and knew that I would learn this method of healing. I had already started to use the power of my love and the power of my breath to help others I would encounter. It was something which I just started doing because I felt it intuitively. And on the weekend after this event, I took my first Reiki healing course. On subsequent weekends, I took the more advanced Reiki courses. Unbeknownst to me I had become a healer once again.

One of my favorite movies is the original Karate Kid. In that movie, Daniel LaRusso, who recently moved to California from New Jersey, is continuously tormented by some Karate bullies and is rescued and subsequently trained by his apartment complex's maintenance man who also happens to be a karate master. The story line culminates in a karate tournament where Daniel is to compete against the bullies, one of who strikes an illegal low blow to Daniel's leg, injuring him severely and seemingly putting him out of the tournament final. Mr. Myagi once again comes to the boy's aid and heals his injured leg with his hands. When I saw this on the screen I thought to myself: "Wow, wouldn't it be great if we could really do that". Little did I know what was in store for me. We really can do that and a whole lot more.

When I got home at the end of the first Reiki class, I was anxious to use my newfound skills. I offered to work on my wife Jill, but she wasn't really interested and said I could work on her the following day, which I did. As I began my journey along the spiritual path, I would often try to share with Jill what I was doing or what I had learned. But she seemed disinterested, and I felt she was only humoring me whenever I told her about my spiritual experiences, although there were times when she would feel impatient or even threatened. She seemed as if she were waiting for this new phase, this new activity to pass after I mastered it, as I had done so many times before in other things. The only willing participant for a healing from me was my mother in law, Alicia, who had always been into new age type stuff, although never too intensely.

Later in the week I found my son Timmy sitting in the kitchen nursing a sore elbow. Timmy was a basketball player as was his older brother Michael. They both played for the Benjamin School in North Palm Beach, Timmy on the Junior Varsity and Mike on the Varsity. I offered to help Timmy and, after assuring him that I really thought I could help him, he said okay. I took his elbow in my two hands, invoked the energies of healing to come into them, and I began to breathe in the life force energy that is everywhere. His eyes got wide as my hands became hot and the energy began to flow into his elbow. It flowed like this for a few minutes and then it just stopped, much like it often did when the healing was complete. Tim was quite surprised about it all, particularly since the pain was gone and he had complete freedom of movement. He smiled, thanked me, and disappeared.

Half an hour later my son Michael showed up and told me that Timmy had told him what happened with him. He asked if I could work on his right shoulder which had been hurting both him and his jump shot. And again, in my best Mr. Myagi fashion, I invoked the healing energies once more and they came through. Michael also received a healing for his shoulder, and I was grateful and delighted that I was able to help my children. The next morning, my boys' trainer and bodybuilder Joey D came to see me. He said to me, "Mr. C, I heard what you did for Mike and Tim. I have a big competition this weekend, and my arms are so sore that I can hardly life them. My biceps are strained, maybe torn, and I came here hoping you could help." And so I asked God for his help and I invoked the healing energies for Joey, and his biceps were healed. This event also proved instrumental in changing Joey's life, and of course my own.

I spent the next few months placing my hands upon anyone who would let me. I sense that this is probably the way most healers get their start, by working on their friends, associates, and loved ones. I even began a healing practice in my office, taking away minor headaches and the like. At Disney World a few weeks later, I was sitting at dinner with my family and their friends, next to my son Jason. Jason had developed a cyst in his wrist, and was scheduled to have surgery that week. I asked him if he wanted me to try and help him and he said sure. After preparing myself, I took his wrist into my two hands and I felt the energy start to flow. And then I felt some things I never felt before. There was a pulsing and an undulating movement, as if something was alive and moving around inside his wrist. His eyes got wide and I sensed his concern as I asked him,

"Do you feel that?" And he said, "Yeah I do. What the heck is it?" And I replied, "I don't know, but I do know that it's good." I didn't know much else about these newfound energies except that they worked and that they came from God. All I had to do was ask to be used in an effort to help others, and the energies came through. This is also true for anyone who sincerely wants to be a healer and selflessly help others. God will come and He and His helpers will work through you. All you have to do is ask and be clear and pure in your intentions. Learning a technique is important too. Because it's so available in so many places, Reiki is a good place to start.

CHAPTER SIX

Miracles

In April of that year my father came down with lung cancer, and I started to visit him more often. As his health
and mobility waned, I placed him in a managed-care facil-
ity, and each time I went to visit him I gave him a healing.
My Dad responded very well to these healings and, with the
help of Spirit, I was always able to alleviate his symptoms
like swollen feet, listlessness, breathing difficulties, and
loss of appetite from the chemotherapy. Unfortunately he
wasn't able to heal his thoughts and, because of this, I was
unable to help heal his cancer, and I knew that he would
soon die because of it. So I concentrated on making him
feel better, and on helping him build the energy bridge or
connection between this world and the next. Most people
hang on and are afraid to die because they fear or simply
don't know what's coming after death. I have learned that
it's quite possible and desirable that one can help build
a bridge over to the Astral World, the place we go after
death, which the dying person is then able to use to actually go to their intended place, a place of love and beauty
where they meet and engage with their deceased friends

and loved ones. These visitations would typically happen during sleep. My father would often awaken and ask what happened to his mother and/or brother who had just been "right here". When he finally died, my dad crossed over quickly and without difficulty.

In my experience I have discovered that people are ultimately responsible for their own healing. As healers we can help them, but we are not responsible for them. Many times miracles happen and God's grace comes through, particularly when the person is ready to receive it. And every healing is a successful one, received on many levels, the results of which may be obvious or not so obvious. Generally, all forms of dis-ease, the opposite of ease, are the result of faulty thoughts and negative emotions that have not been healed or dealt with, and which have been reinforced so often that they set themselves up vibrationally in the body in the form of illness or disease. The illness is really the symptom, with the unbalanced and negative thoughts and emotions the true cause. Only the person himself is able to deal with the causes, and gain the understanding and realization necessary to heal them, and it is ultimately each of us who are responsible for ourselves. In many of his healings, the Christ would ask the person who sought healing to say aloud what it was they wanted. This simple act resulted in the person setting his clear intention and demonstrating his faith, and it placed that intention into motion through the use of the spoken word or sound vibration, the creative vibrational force. In western society we want to be fixed. In Spirit we are able to fix ourselves through self-understanding and channeled energies, often with a little help from our friends.

One afternoon after my Dad had become ill, I went to see Pamir, my Reiki instructor, to receive a healing. After the session I was really charged with energy. I was electric. My vibration was so high that I had a hard time holding it, and I could feel my body shaking. That night I had invited my Dad to join me at my house for dinner. My family was away on a trip, and I was home alone, except for our cook Steve, who my wife had recently hired to cook dinner for us. When I arrived home, my father was already there, waiting in the media room next to the kitchen. Steve followed me there as I went in to greet him. As I would typically do these days whenever I met him, I gave my Dad a big hug, filled my heart with love, and then breathed this love into his body. He really loved when I hugged him this way. On this partic-ular day I hugged him for what seemed about ten seconds, and my love moved right into him. He moaned softly as he felt the energy, and I could feel him smile. And then sud-denly, I felt his body go limp in my arms as I heard and felt his lungs deflate in a long moan. His eyes were wide open and blank as I gently set his limp body down upon the sofa. My Father had died in my arms.

Instinctively I knew exactly what to do, and I wondered why I wasn't more upset by this unexpected turn of events. I placed the index and middle finger of my left hand upon his right temple and I started breathing deeply and began to send him energy through my fingers. I started calling him back. "Dad, it's not time yet. You still have things to do, things you must resolve. Come back. Come back." I contin-ued this for a few minutes. The whole time, I could see Steve standing there, mouth wide open, watching intently. Then suddenly, my father jumped up, full of energy, slapped and rubbed his hands together and declared, "Okay, I'm ready to eat. What's for dinner?" Seeing this, Steve freaked out, and took off out of the room like a gunshot. I said to my Father, "Dad, are you okay? How do you feel?" To which he replied, "Man, Charles, I feel great! I haven't felt this good in a long time." And then I asked him, "Dad, do you know what just happened?" He looked a little puzzled at first, but then he replied, "Uh, oh yeah, that. Well I was just resting, but now I'm back". I said, "Are you sure you're okay. Do you want to sit down for a while?" And he said, "Charles, I'm fine. I don't know what you're talking about". And with that he bolted for the kitchen, full of vim and vigor, as I trailed behind him.

In the kitchen I found Steve huddled in a corner, white as a ghost, his body trembling uncontrollably. I placed my hand on his heart to calm him down and I asked him, "Steve, are you all right?" He had difficulty composing himself at first, and then he asked, "Did, did, did what I see happen in there, just happen in there?" I thought about my answer for a moment before giving it, and I said simply, "Steve, you were there along with me. What do you think happened?" And Steve replied nearly hysterically, "He died and came back, right? I saw it. He did, didn't he?" And I answered, "Yes, he did." And then I said, "Well Steve, he's okay now and everything's fine, so why don't we all sit down together and eat". That night my Dad and I, along with Steve, ate dinner together. I never saw Steve again after that. Later, after they had left, I realized fully what had actually trans- pired. I felt so very blessed that God had allowed me to receive this blessing this night and impart it to my Dad, and I wondered and was excited about what was in store for me in the future. I also considered whether I was up to the tests and challenges that I knew would be coming.

On July 23rd, I had my forty-eighth birthday. I stopped and reflected that day on all the things that had happened to me during this past year, and how much I and my life had changed. So many things had occurred that I could hardly keep track of them, and everything was leading up to some big event, I was sure, although I didn't know what this could possibly be. Despite all that had come to pass, I still hadn't mastered my own ego, and my newfound spiritual self continued to wrestle with the warrior who still came out in me every now and then. A few days after my birthday, I received a call from Scott Krinsky, my brother-in-law and director of our store operations. Scott called to talk about our business, and also to tell me about his brother-in-law's newborn baby, and how she was expected to die at any time. The infant was in the Pediatric Intensive Care Unit at St. Mary's Hospital in West Palm Beach. The child, born three months prematurely on the same day as I was, July 23rd, had a contusion of the brain that was bleeding freely, and the hospital was powerless to stop it. They said that the baby was unable to produce enough stems cells for the brain to heal itself, and that her demise was inevitable. I took the fact that the baby and I were both born on the same day as a sign. After we talked for a while I said to Scott, "Scott, maybe I can help her." To which he replied, "Well brother, that's what I was hoping you'd say." I arranged to meet him that evening at the hospital. Because it was the Intensive Care Unit, only direct relatives of the patient were allowed to visit. But we decided to play it by ear and see what happened.

I arrived at the hospital at about 7:30 that evening. There to meet me were Scott, and Stuart and Julie, the parents of the child, both of whom I knew. I could see the worry and concern in their eyes as they feared for the life of their child. I told them that we would do the best we could to help their baby, that we would call upon God's love to come through and assist us, and I asked them to pray. As I prepared myself for the healing, I felt an energy come into and flow through me that I had never felt before. It was powerful, focused, and yet so gentle all at the same time. In my mind I heard the name Mother Mary, and I realized that she was the one who had come to help. And I thought to myself that I must have done something really good in some other lifetime for all the blessings I have received in this one.

When I entered the ICU, no one seemed to notice me; not the duty nurse, not the nurse attending the infants, no one. It was as if I was the invisible man. The child, whose name was Kelly, was in an incubator, and you could see how much she was struggling. The poor little thing was so tiny, so vulnerable. She was all scrunched up and moving around uncomfortably, as if she were totally unhappy in her body and searching for the peace that eluded her. As her parents watched, I began speaking to her telepathically, telling her that I had come to help her and that I was her friend. Besides, we even have something in common, I told her, we were born on the same day. I asked for God's healing light to come through me and to flow to her. There were two round openings in the incubator through which I could place my hands, one at the head and another at the feet.

But before placing my hands inside, I hesitated, as I thought of what had happened to my father the previous day at my home, and I was reluctant to touch the infant. Sensing my hesitation, I could hear Mary say to me, "Go ahead, Charles." I hesitated for a moment, but I felt the energy come in, and so I began the healing. I placed my left hand inside the incubator and held it open-palmed about three inches above her head. Immediately I felt the energy flowing through my hand and into the child. She started to squirm even more now and she looked more uncomfortable than ever. In my mind I heard a voice say, "It's okay beloved, keep going." And after a short while, I placed my other hand inside the incubator too, a few inches below her feet. And true to form, the energy began to flow into her feet as well. You could tell she felt this too, as she reacted even more uncomfortably. And then suddenly she just relaxed into the energy and the tension in her body just melted away. She looked so beautiful and at peace in that moment and I noticed there was a faint smile on her face. Where before she had seemed so troubled, now she was angelic. My heart leapt when I saw this.

A sense of peace and serenity now descended over the both of us. I moved my left hand and placed it directly on the top of her head, lightly touching her. In a few minutes I moved my right hand onto the soles of her feet. The energy was really flowing now, and she was just absorbing it all and drinking it up. I wondered how she could take it all, for the energy was very powerful and gentle at the same time. I stood there motionless for what must have been at least an hour, channeling the energy to this sweet little girl, and visualizing the formation of stem cells to clot her blood. And then it was finished. Just as suddenly as it had begun, the energy just stopped, and I knew in that instant that she was going to be okay. When I went over to the parents and told them not to worry, I saw the questioning look in their faces, searching my eyes to see if what I said could be true. I said, "Really. Don't worry. She's going to be just fine. I promise. She's a special little child and she will have a normal life. They will be releasing her from the hospital in twenty-one days." Sensing the truth of what I told them, they thanked me profusely as they both began to cry. When they asked me how they could ever thank me enough I told them simply, "Just thank God for the wonderful gift he has given you". Exactly twenty-one days later, the child was released from the hospital.

Today Kelly is a beautiful teenage girl, full of energy. Although she's had some residual effects from the brain injury, she has lived the life of any other normal child. Sometime later, long after the healing, I learned that one of the delivery room nurses had dropped her on her head, and this had been the cause of the cranial bleeding. Another nurse, unable to live with the guilt, had come forward and revealed what had happened.

CHAPTER SEVEN

A Change Is Gonna Come, Oh Yes It Will

Can you believe it? The things I was going through, seeing, and experiencing were incredible, unbelievable, and yet I felt so comfortable. Because I felt things, things I had never felt before, I knew they were real and true. The astrologer had told me that all the events in my life were leading up to something significant. I knew change was coming, but I didn't know exactly what or how it would play out. I was concerned, concerned for my family, for my company, and for my employees. I was also concerned I wasn't up the task. I had a mission and a purpose. That was for certain. God had said to me that October day, "You will know everything, when it's time". Sometimes you just don't want to know. But I was committed, no matter what.

After my first visit to Awakenings, I would go there often, looking for a new book, a new piece of music, a new workshop, or a new experience. One Friday evening I stopped by after work to pick up some cassette tapes Karen had ordered for me. As I was paying for my purchase, she suggested that I should stick around. She told me she had a wonderful reader coming in that night, and she felt that I would really enjoy it if I stayed. Naturally I wanted to stay. But I couldn't give her the answer I wanted, because I knew that my wife Jill would not go for it. She viewed my newfound interest in spirituality and healing with a great deal of skepticism and mistrust. I often chose not to venture out at all, rather than upset her. I told Karen that I would really like to stay but that it wasn't possible. Maybe another time. Although I was reluctant to call Jill and tell her what I wanted to do, I decided to try anyway, even though I was certain of her reaction. I went outside, dialed home on my cell phone, and I asked her if she would mind if I stayed for the readings. She responded, "Sure honey, no problem. Have a good time. I'll see you afterwards." Even though my mouth dropped open and I wondered who that was on the other end of the call, I thanked her and told her I would be home about nine. This was the first time she had ever given her consent freely, and I was really quite surprised. I went back into the store to browse around and wait for the reader who was coming at seven. The reader's name was Gloriana Peale.

When Gloriana arrived fifteen minutes later, ten people were there waiting, including me. I was the only man. She greeted everybody in a warm friendly manner and I instantly took a liking to her. She seemed so very familiar to me, like someone I had known before, like a sister or close friend perhaps, and I immediately felt comfortable with her and with her energy. The group formed their chairs in a circle with Gloriana in the center, and we began our guided

meditation. It was a beautiful meditation where we followed a mountain path which led up to a beautiful temple,
the Temple of the Higher Self. There we were able to meet
and communicate with that greater aspect of ourselves,
our Spirit or God-Self. It was pretty incredible. After the
meditation, Gloriana went around the circle giving each of
us a message that she had received.

I was one of the last to receive a message, and when she
came to me she said, "Charles, I see the woman you are
going to be with the rest of your life. She's thirty-seven
years old, blond, thin, and her light shines very bright". At
that exact moment I saw her too and I said to Gloriana,
"Oh my, I see her too!" What I saw so clearly was the pro-
file of a younger woman, who I was sure I didn't know but
who seemed so familiar. I saw her as if in a dream, only
clearer, except I couldn't quite make out her face. Her hair
was cut short and she looked both regal and mystical. The
one feature that struck me was the slight crook or bend of
her nose, and for the next few months I looked everywhere
for this thin, short-haired, thirty-seven year old blonde
woman with the crooked nose, to no avail. Finally I just
stopped looking and resigned myself to my fate, whatever
that would be. For I really wasn't looking for another, I was
too busy searching for myself.

In the beginning of 1996, my Goldman Sachs partners
wanted to put Tire Kingdom up for sale. They told me
they'd had a lot of interest, particularly from Sears, and
that we could make a great deal, that it was a slam dunk.
I thought "Wow, isn't God wonderful. He's even settling
the Tire Kingdom issue for me and allowing me a graceful

exit". I read that one wrong, as just the opposite happened. Sears had their own problems and we pared the
negotiations down to one suitor who wouldn't or perhaps
couldn't pay the price my partners wanted. Putting a company through a sale takes a great deal out of it. Business
suffered, our employees were insecure, and I turned in my
notice, agreeing to work for the remaining nine months left
on my contract. A few weeks later, my partners scheduled
a visit to come down and meet with me privately, during
the first week of August. I really didn't think much of this at
that moment, other than to recognize that they had something up their sleeves. The real understanding would come
to me soon afterwards.

I had been reading a wonderful little channeled book called
The Impersonal Life, and that night and the following morning I finished it, the same day I was to meet my partners.
The book speaks to you directly from God. Many say that
each reading of the book gives, and each person reading
it receives, something different, something personal. The
book is about entering the spiritual life and the spiritual
path, and is a primer on what that means. Each of us are
all a part of the same Oneness, the same consciousness.
Each of us possesses the Christ Consciousness within our
hearts, the perfected state of human existence, and each
of us is a son or daughter of God, a Christ in the making, if
we so choose to follow the spiritual path. The main difference between a born-again Christian and a spiritual person
on the Path of Christ Consciousness is that the Christian is
looking to be "saved" by something outside of themselves,
by Jesus, while the spiritually 'aware' person understands
that God or Christ Consciousness comes from within. When

I finished reading, I asked for wisdom and clarity, so that I could accept what was coming with grace and understanding. In order to enter the spiritual path, the spiritual life, each of us must go through a crucifixion of sorts, where our old life ends and a new life begins, and our old personality dies and a new one is reborn. Just like the Christ, we are resurrected. We are resurrected from separation and ignorance into spiritual connection and awareness. I knew then that my own crucifixion, the crucifixion of my old ego/personality was imminent. To travel the spiritual path requires the initiate to depart from their old lives and circumstances in order to make way for the new. In life, in relationship, in Spirit, the old must pass out before the new can come in.

I drove to work that morning and waited in my office for my partners to arrive. They were due in about eleven o'clock. I had already called my lawyer and friend, Jerry Cantor, and I asked him to come to my office. I knew what was going to happen, and I was sure that I would need him today. My son Michael came by to visit me at 10am. I was surprised to see Mike and I asked him why he had come. He told me he was thinking about me, and he just wanted to come by to see me and to see how I was doing. It was unlike Mike to come and visit me, particularly in the morning. It was like he sensed something was up. I told Mike what was in store for me this day. I told him that in a little while my partners would be here to fire me, and this would be my last day at Tire Kingdom. When he asked me what I was going to do, I told him that it was time for me to go now, that I had accomplished everything I had set out to do, and my life was now leading me somewhere else. He said, "Dad, that's so

unlike you. I know you could kick their butts if you wanted."
I smiled with the understanding that my children had always known me as a fighter. "I don't want to Mike", was my
reply. "I know that God has something important planned
for me to do, and it's no longer about being the Tire King.
So I'm going to accept it, make the best deal I can, and
go quietly without a fight. Besides, I was leaving anyway."
Mike said, "Dad, maybe it's not what you think." When I assured him that it was exactly what I thought, he said, "Well
Dad, you always do what is right. I love you and I'm proud
of you." Out of the mouths of babes. I hugged and kissed
him and told him I loved him too. And then I thanked him
for coming to see me and said I would see him that night. I
really needed a friend this day, and it was my eighteen year
old son who showed up at just the right moment.

The partners arrived at about eleven fifteen. I greeted
them in the parking lot and invited them into my office.
They were noticeably nervous and uneasy. When I tried
to make eye contact with them neither of them would look
me in the eye. We exchanged pleasantries, and made small
talk for a few minutes. One told me that they wanted to
interview and speak with each member of the upper man-
agement team separately to get their views on what the
company needed. The other suggested that afterwards,
we could go off site and meet together. They had already
booked a meeting room at a nearby hotel. I just smiled,
which seemed to make them more nervous, and then I told
them I would make the arrangements. It was clear what
they were up to, and I already knew what was going down.

After three hours of interviewing, they came back to my

office and asked if I was ready to go off with them for our meeting. I smiled and said, "Gentlemen, I know why you're here and what you want to do. There's no need to go any-where. I'm going to make it easy on you, and we can do the whole thing right here. Really, it's no problem." They were shocked at this to say the least. In the past I would have acted much differently. Instead, they didn't even have to say the words, as I was the one who broke the ice. I could feel the power of Spirit moving within me, and I knew that I was in good hands. We went down to the conference room to work out the details of my severance.

I negotiated a really good severance package, one that I'm surprised they agreed to, considering the fact that initially they had wanted me to continue to do the company com-mercials and to serve as a consultant in exchange for the severance package, something I first considered and then refused to do. I told them that once I was gone, I had to be free. After some negotiation, they agreed to give me the severance anyway. Later, after they left and we said good-bye, my lawyer Jerry Cantor asked me how in the world I was able to do what I did, and to get them to agree to what they did. He said, "Chuck, that was masterful how you were able to turn this whole thing around on them". I said, "Jerry, I didn't do a thing. You were here and you saw what happened. I did nothing except to follow my heart. What you witnessed here today was the Universe at work. They have a different purpose for me now and they were helping me to get out." And then I realized the impact of what truly did happen and I said, "It was incredible, wasn't it?" And Jerry looked into my eyes, smiled and said, "Yes it was."

And so we agreed and the deal was done. Tom Garvey, the Chief Financial Officer and my successor as acting President, signed the agreement on behalf of the company. Tom had been undermining me with our Board of Directors for some time, while maneuvering for himself the role as my successor. Surprisingly, I wasn't upset with him in the least. I simply looked him in the eye and said, "One day you will have to atone for your actions and for what you've done here." His mouth dropped and he just looked at me. Although he was well aware of his own actions, what he didn't realize was that he had been the unknowing instrument of Spirit. Even though he was motivated by selfish reasons and self-interest, the effect of his actions were to free me from the chains that bound me, and allow me to move forward with my spiritual purpose. So many times in life, even though a person does something untoward and suffers the karmic ramifications of his actions, he is still the unwitting instrument of Spirit.

When I told my employees in a hastily called meeting that I was retiring from the company, they reacted with shock and dismay. Many of them started crying and I realized how much so many of them cared for and depended on me. Holding back my tears, I told them how grateful I was to each of them for the hard work, devotion, and caring they had all invested into Tire Kingdom. I explained to them that, after all, it was the people who made the company what it was, and that without them, Tire Kingdom was just a collection of bricks and mortar, and inventory. And I assured them not to worry, to do their best, and that everything would be fine. My whole world, and theirs, had changed in an instant. And so I said goodbye to the company and to the people I had loved so much. Afterwards, many of them came up to me to thank me for all that I had done for them and for giving them the opportunities to grow and to learn and to be more than ordinary. I went home that night with a grateful and a heavy heart. As tough as this was, other things remained to be done in the ensuing months that would be even tougher.

The next day the story broke in the daily newspapers. And even though we intentionally did not send press releases to TV stations, one TV station, WPBF 25, requested and came to my office to do an interview. And even though I'd already had an emotional episode with my employees the day before, this one really surprised me. The reporter was a young woman, born and raised in West Palm Beach, who like so many others, had grown up watching me on TV. She took me back in time to where I started Tire Kingdom in the Farmer's Market with less than five hundred dollars, and how impossible it all seemed back then to succeed. She related to me how so many had watched and loved our commercials over decades, and how impressed she was with our growth and our success. I thanked her for her kind and considerate words, and then I went on air to thank the many people and the many customers who had made Tire Kingdom and me a success over the years. I expressed my heartfelt gratitude to them and I thanked them for everything. And I began to weep and to smile at the same time, as I realized how many blessings and how many good things had been given to me in my tenure with Tire Kingdom. I had created the company from noth-ing, achieved great success, and I had lived the American Dream. There were no more battles to fight, no enemies to conquer, nothing left to prove, and nothing left to do. I'd had a good run, and now it was time to let go, and to move on to the really important things in life.

And so without acknowledgement, congratulations, recognition, or even a plaque to commemorate the event, I was discharged from the company I had built and loved, and from the life I had known these past twenty-four years, virtually to the day. But I was happy and the better for it, because I knew that this was my path, and the new could not come in until the old had departed. On Friday August 8th, I cleaned out my office completely. The next day I got on the plane for Delphi, and the beginning of my new life. And I never looked back.

CHAPTER EIGHT

Delphi

Delphi University is a unique and astonishing place, unlike any other in the world. Here we live the Archimedean Principle of turning the lead of humanity into the gold of the Divine. Located on a peninsula surrounded by a white water river, in a protected enclave which had served as the ceremonial grounds of the Cherokee Nation for thousands of years, Delphi is a university of higher spiritual learning. Founded by Patricia Hayes in 1974, and continued and expanded with her husband Marshall Smith, a former Executive Vice President with Kimberly-Clark Paper Company, Delphi provides the spiritual seeker with a true spiritual education, direct spiritual experience, personal healing, and self-empowerment. Students who come here learn how to discover, access, develop, refine, and express their spiritual gifts and abilities. They learn how to heal themselves and others, and how to overcome their own shadows and their lower nature. Most of the ones who study at Delphi enter into service to God and mankind.

The day after my retirement, I was scheduled to head out

on the plane to Atlanta, and from there take the two hour van ride up into the Blue Ridge Mountains of North Georgia and the Delphi Center. I was going to Delphi to take a one week course called In-Depth Channeling. All I knew about the one week intensive course was that we would learn to become channels of spiritual energies. I was very excited about coming to Delphi. After the spinning brochure event which prompted me to register, and the obvious synchronicity and timing between my retirement and my already scheduled departure the next day, I knew that there was something special about Delphi, and that Spirit was leading me there as my next step. I remembered what the astrologer had told me, that I would encounter and meet those people who were to assist me on my path over the spring and summer months, and this would all culminate in late July and early August. I also remembered another thing she said that, throughout my existence, I had always been right on time, never early and never late, but always on time. That certainly was an accurate description of what was happening now.

We were greeted at the airport by the Delphi administrator, Steve Smith, and once everyone had arrived, we boarded two vans for the two hour trip north to Delphi, outside of the old copper mining town of McCaysville, Georgia, located at the point on the map where the states of Georgia, Tennessee, and North Carolina all come together. There were seven of us in the airport group, six women and me. Ultimately, our class would total eleven people in all, eight woman and three men. Although this is gradually changing, there are typically many more women involved in spiritual pursuits than there are men, and our group was no different. The others in our group were driving in and we would meet them later at Delphi. The ride up was spectacular. We left the city, traveled through the foothills, and on up into the mountains in our journey to this place of Light. We spent the trip introducing ourselves, talking about our spiritual experiences, and laughing and joking. Although I previously had few women friends in my life, I was quickly becoming comfortable not only being around and talking with women, but with my own sensitivity as well. I felt very comfortable with this group of Mediumship students, and I felt that I had known some of them in the past. Later I would discover how true this really was.

At Delphi we teach and do amazing things, and the initiates who come here learn to access their true spiritual gifts and abilities, and to heal themselves. Delphi is a modern day Mystery School, similar in many ways to the ancient schools of spiritual learning that existed in places like Egypt, Greece, Northern Europe, Tibet, India, China, and South America. The mystery schools have preserved, protected, revealed, and expanded the true and accurate spiritual teachings of God throughout the history of man. Over the doorways of virtually all the Ancient Mystery Schools is inscribed this basic and fundamental instruction to each initiate who would follow the path of Self-discovery: "Know Thyself".

When the disciples asked the Christ how they could know him better, he replied, "Know Yourselves". And when they pressed him on what they should do after that, he replied, "Know yourselves some more." What the Christ and the Mystery Schools taught was a fundamental truth, one that has been known throughout the ages by the privileged few.

If you truly want to discover God, you will find him within your own heart. For each of us is a part of God, and God is within each of us. The search for God is the search for Self; the search for Self is the search for God.

At Delphi, Patricia Hayes and staff have not only carried forward the esoteric teachings of the ages, but they have also brought through many new and revolutionary spiritual techniques such as Mediumship training, numerous new healing methods such as energy healing, color and sound healing, etheric reflective healing, inner child healing, and the revolutionary RoHun™ spiritual psychotherapy process of mental and emotional healing. These are just a few of the incredible and powerful healing techniques one can learn and experience at Delphi.

All things that exist, exist as some form of energy, from the earth itself and all its parts, to all the life forms that inhabit it. From the air we breathe to the sunlight that illuminates and warms the planet, from the invisible like electricity to the obvious like lightning, even your thoughts and feelings, all things exist as a form of energy. The fundamental difference between one form of energy and another is its density and rate of vibration. At Delphi, the first thing one learns is to read, perceive, channel, and direct energy in its many forms. In order to increase one's perception and access one's own spiritual abilities, one must connect with one's Higher Consciousness or Higher Self. One begins and enhances this connection through meditation, through the setting of one's intention to tap into the power of the God-Self, and by devoting the time and effort each day to do so. Every day at Delphi begins with morning meditation, where each of us can make the energetic connection with God and our own Higher Selves. It's the perfect way to start the day, and, if you truly want to access these abilities and walk the spiritual path, the only way.

There are three experiential classes scheduled each day during the In-Depth Channeling week, and we are kept busy from morning until night learning, building, and developing our spiritual and energetic perception and abilities. Each class helps one to develop and enhance their channeling abilities and their spiritual sensitivities of clairvoyance (the ability to see psychically), clairsentience (the ability to feel psychically), clairaudience (the ability to hear psychically), and others. These are abilities possessed by every human being in varying degrees and in various levels of development. The word Psychic means simply, 'the Breath of God'. During these class sessions, we also spent a lot of time gaining insight about ourselves, and clearing and healing many of those lower energies that hold us and keep us from expressing our true light.

I felt so very comfortable here. It was as if I had come home, and everyone in the class felt the same way. I was amazed at how much we all learned, and how fast we learned it. Within two days we were giving each other basic psychic readings, interpreting psychic energy, and channeling healing through our hands and through our breath, something I never dreamed possible. Each of us has a great many spiritual abilities, most of which lie latent within us. It is simply a matter of connecting with our Spirit, setting our intention to develop these abilities, asking for assistance from above, and finding a place to facilitate that development. There is no better place on earth for this than Delphi University.

One of the early classes for psychic development at Delphi is the Psychic Art Class. In this class, each of us was paired with a partner, and we were tasked to draw a psychic picture of our partner using colored chalks while blindfolded. The pictures we drew were not portraits, but were energetic representations of the person. We used multiple colors of different chalks and we picked them intuitively, so that none of us knew what colors the pictures were going to be, or what any of them looked like until we were completely finished and removed our blindfolds. Then each of us would "read" the portrait we drew and tell our partner what it meant about them. The purpose of the exercise was to access and increase our sensitivity to energy in one of its many forms.

The instructor of this class was Kimberly Hayes Panisset, the daughter of Delphi school founder Patricia Hayes. Kimberly had already taught one other class since we arrived, and today she was instructing us on how to draw the psychic portraits. She was now going around the room asking and helping us to interpret our pictures for each other. When Kimberly came to us, my partner asked her for help in interpreting the picture she had drawn of me. Kimberly looked at the picture, paused for a moment, and then said, "Oh my God. There's a woman who loves this man and she doesn't even know it". Immediately I felt certain that Kimberly was talking about herself. But I dismissed it away just as quickly as she said it. I mean, after all, how could that be right? She was a goddess, and I was a novice, and we really didn't know each other, or so I thought. How could she possibly be in love with me?

Throughout the week we learned, practiced, and developed our channeling and spiritual abilities. And along the way we developed great friendships with each other. Because we were all together, revealing our thoughts, emotions, feelings, deepest secrets, and vulnerabilities, we soon became the best of friends. We learned to know each other far better perhaps than we knew anyone else, even our closest friends, and we were in a safe place with a supportive group of enlightened people with whom we all felt comfortable and who we trusted. It's like that at Delphi. Each class that assembles here comes together for a unique purpose, and the members of each class all have something in common. This may be a past life connection, a current life issue, emotion, condition, or limitation they all share, or some other connection such as fear, abuse, or power issues. At Delphi we not only learned how to use our spiritual gifts, but each of us were also able to receive healing for many of those lower energies that held us captive and kept us from expressing our true light.

On Wednesday of that week, we were privileged to experience a trance channeling from Marshall Smith, Patricia Hayes' husband and one of the co-founders of Delphi. Marshall trance channels Arthur Ford, the late great psychic of Harry Houdini and international fame, and Patricia's former boss. It was Arthur who brought back Houdini's message from beyond the grave and recited it verbatim to Houdini's wife Beatrice, who confirmed the authenticity of the message. It was also Arthur who gave Delphi the method and the techniques for the In-Depth Channeling course we still teach. Patricia received these channeled instructions directly from Arthur *after* his death. As with most trance channels, Marshall would leave his body and allow Arthur to come in and use it to speak with us. Arthur was quite a character. His easy humor and laughter put us all at ease as we asked him questions about life after death, the status of our loved ones, and the meaning of existence. When we asked what we all had in common as a group, Arthur told us that we had started the Huguenot Revolt in Southern France in the Sixteenth Century, and that although we were originally fourteen in number, three of the fourteen were currently in-between lives.

The entire week at Delphi was extraordinary. We worked morning, noon, and night. All of the classes, all of the work we did, were leading up to the big event. We spent all of Friday afternoon giving readings to each other. Then on Friday evening, ready or not, the big event had come. We were surprised to learn that each of us was to give two psychic readings to two different people that evening, all of whom were strangers. Only a few of us were suffering anxiety about this. Of course I was one of these. What also added to the pressure was that we heard that a group of RoHun™ Doctors, who were also here studying, were going to sit for some of the readings. As luck would have it, both of my clients were Doctors of RoHun™. Although I was really nervous, I took a deep breath and allowed the energy to flow, and did what I had learned to do all week. And the readings turned out great.

A person who channels psychic information often feels like their making it up, usually because the information comes so easily, or that it's so far-fetched that it just couldn't be right. It is during these times that doubt, the killer of psychic ability, appears. It's because we all inherently possess these natural gifts and abilities in varying degrees and levels of development that the information often comes or seems easy. It's easy because it's supposed to come that way, easily. Being psychic is our natural state. And when something is revealed that seems as if it couldn't possibly be right, that's when you must trust your feelings, for it almost always is. Trust is the opposite of doubt, and keeps you in the channel of energy. If you're in the energy, you get the information, for the information comes on the energy. You access this energy through your intention and your breath.

The first person I read for was having difficulties in her own life, and the advice and love she needed simply flowed through me to her. Her tears and her gratitude said it all. My next client, a very gifted and experienced RoHun psychotherapist, was trying to decide where and how to set up her spiritual practice. After detailing her past lives in Asia and the Pacific, as well as her current intentions, I was able to channel the solutions and the advice from Spirit to her as well, advising her to choose Boulder over Sedona, the truth of which she felt and followed. Every one of my classmates fared as well. It was an unbelievable climax to an unbelievable week. That night we all celebrated our new-found spiritual success and we prepared to say goodbye the next day. All but two of our classmates were scheduled to return home, myself included.

Early the next morning, I sought out Patricia and asked her if I could stay for the Advanced Channeling course that was to begin that evening. She told me the class was very full, with twenty six people in all, but that she would try to work it out for me. I really wanted to stay for this course, as it included such things as Trance Healing, Past Life Regression, the Astral Plane, and the Healings of the Christ, things which I wanted to learn how to do, and which were related to my previous spiritual experience. Later that morning, Patricia told me that they were going to split the class into two groups, and that I was welcome to attend. I was elated. I was really into God, Spirit, and now Delphi, in ways that I never knew existed. I knew and felt the truth of these things, and I was thirsty for more. I was very sad to say goodbye to my Channeling class. They were my dear friends with whom I'd become very close, and I was sad to see them go. They had been so supportive of me and they helped me to see things about my life and myself more clearly than I ever had before. Two of them would help me again, a few months later.

That night we began the Advanced Channeling course, now known as the Healing Mysteries. Although sad that so many of my friends had departed, this next class was also a great group, as all classes at Delphi are, and I soon made new friends and acquaintances, although nothing can compare to the experience and the uniqueness of the In-Depth Channeling week. All of us had transformed, from what we were to what we were becoming. But of all the courses I have taken at Delphi, the Healing Mysteries is and would remain my favorite. In this class we took our channeling abilities and expanded them to a new level. We learned how to scan and screen a person's physical, mental, and emotional bodies, and to determine the source and the causes of imbalance and disease within that person and, in my own case, right down to specific things like the person's leukocyte count and which of their children was the cause of their emotional upset. In essence we learned how to become medical intuitives, but what was really interesting is that all we were given was the first name of the person and their age. The rest we had to do for ourselves. In addition to so many other things we learned, we were also instructed on how to perform Past Life regressions, and we did multiple sessions on each other. In one lifetime I was a holy man in Israel with a message for the king. In another I was a scientist on the ancient continent of Lemuria. We also learned how to do distance healing and to send healing energy to others who weren't even present, and who in many cases were thousands of miles away. What was this magical place called Delphi, where ordinary people learned to do such incredible and extraordinary things?

Although I loved learning how to psychically scan another person, how to project my healing energy over great distances, or to perform Past Life Regression, what I liked best about this course was learning the technique of Trance Healing, a technique I have practiced and expanded upon in my own healing practice. Although similar to Reiki, Trance Healing is not only about bringing through healing energies to help others. In this form of healing, other spiritual beings called Spirit Doctors also work with you to assist the person on your healing table. Typically, a Spirit Doctor is a being who worked in healing when they were incarnate, usually as a doctor or nurse or spiritual healer, and who now continues their healing work from the other side. When experiencing this type of healing, people often report feeling multiple hands touching them during the healing. Although one may think that this is enough to freak any-body out, the energy of love that accompanies the healing just doesn't allow for feelings of fear to occur. Where there is light, there is no darkness. What is really awesome is that we were not only privileged to work with a complement of Spirit Doctors, we were able to meet them personally. Some of us even learned their names and also saw what they looked like. When I received my first healing from my partner Suban, who was also in my Channeling class, I could feel her hands very physically upon my head, and at the same time I could feel other hands holding my feet. To my surprise Suban was working there and the Spirit Doctor was working on my head. I was sure that I would find it the other way around, because I could feel the touch more significantly at my head than I could feel it at my feet.

At the end of the week, we were each given a different per-son on whom to perform a Trance Healing. These people were local folks from around the area who were in need of physical healing. My client was a sixty-eight year old man named Pratt Beavers. Pratt had been in a serious auto ac-cident a few weeks beforehand and, as a result, had been pronounced permanently blind by three different doctors. Fortunately for him, Kimberly Panisset had been able to restore his eyesight. But he still had other lingering prob-lems such as an injured back and a dislocated shoulder that wouldn't heal. They gave Pratt to me because they all felt that I had and could channel the kind of strong and directive spleen energy needed to effect his healing. Pratt received a wonderful healing that evening and much of his pain and symptoms were gone for good. I also received something too, as I always do whenever I perform a healing. In Healing Mysteries I had learned a new technique and a new way to help others. And more importantly, I had become a better channel and a better healer myself.

The following morning was the last day of class. As we typically did after the end of a class, we all met in the main teaching room to share our experiences and for a closing ceremony and the award of certifications in the course of study we had just completed. Patricia Hayes was conducting the ceremony, and we were all so happy at all that we had done and learned. At the same time we were all a little sad and bummed out about leaving. Patricia was talking when she stopped abruptly and said, "Oh by the way everybody, say Happy Birthday to Kimberly. It's her thirty-eighth birthday". Patricia's daughter Kimberly had just walked into the room. I was facing forward on a sofa, and when I turned to look at Kimberly, I wasn't prepared for what I saw. Prior to this day, Kimberly had extremely long hair, extending well below her shoulders, and had always worn it down. But on this day she had her hair pinned up on her head. And when I turned to look at her, who should be standing there but the thin and now thirty-eight year old blond-haired woman with the little bend in her nose, the very same one I had seen in my vision at the Awakenings Bookstore! My mouth just dropped, and I was stunned. There she was, bigger than life, the woman with whom I was supposed to spend the rest of my life. How was it that I hadn't been able to 'see' her before?

When class ended I went over to Kimberly and asked if I could speak with her for a moment. I had no idea what I was going to say. So when we went outside, I just told her. I said, "Kimberly, I know this is going to sound crazy, and I know you must get a lot of this from other men, but some months ago a psychic told me told me that I would meet the woman with whom I would spend the rest of my life. And I think that person is you." Oh brother, I thought. I couldn't believe I just said that. Kimberly's eyes penetrated into my own for what seemed an eternity and then she said: "That's funny you say that, because two different people also told me something similar, that I would meet the man I would spend the rest of my life with, here at Delphi, in August". Kimberly then related to me that her plan had been to move with her children to Portugal the following week and take a job teaching children there. But upon learning of her plans, one of the students in the Advanced Channeling class, Ariana, had told her emphatically, "Don't Go!" The student didn't know why she was telling Kimberly this, only that she was being directed very strongly by spirit to do so. Kimberly felt the strength of Ariana's convictions, meditated on it, and cancelled her plans to go overseas.

Neither I nor Kimberly reacted to these things that could only be considered synchronistic at the very least, and we spent the next twenty minutes talking, talking easily and comfortably with each other. We were like two old friends who'd had a chance meeting, and who were now catching up on lost time. I felt so comfortable in her energy, and she in mine. We didn't really talk about anything specific, nor were either of us surprised about this turn of events, which in itself was surprising. Soon her brother Sterling, who also worked at the school, told me I had better get my things packed as the last van was leaving shortly. I told Kimberly I would say goodbye before I left, and Sterling accompanied me to my room to help me pack. As we were packing my suitcase I said to Sterling, "Sterling, I think I'm falling in love with your sister." To which he answered, "Ah, don't worry about that. Everybody falls in love with her."

Sterling and I carried my bags to the van together and loaded them into the back. Kimberly was standing there hugging and saying goodbye to the others as they filed into the van. The last seat available was the front passenger seat. Before I got in, I hugged her and then I looked into her eyes and said simply, "I have some things I have to take care of." As I was getting into the van, I turned to look at her again as she looked back at me. And then I really saw her. I could feel my heart sink, for I had said goodbye to her like this before, on a roadside in ancient Greece. We were both very young then and deeply in love. I was leaving to go to war, a war from which I never returned, having been killed in battle. And here I found myself once more, saying goodbye to her again. As the van pulled away, our eyes were riveted on each other. We realized so much in just a moment.

During the two hour drive to the airport I was entranced. I just didn't know what to think or feel or do. And so I did nothing. I had learned enough about Spirit to know that these things would unfold in the way they were meant to, and in the way they had been planned. Many months later, Patricia would tell us that she had observed us that day on the road. She said the two of us had spheres of white light moving between our heart chakras as we stood facing each other. She knew then that Kimberly and I were destined to be together. I did too, but I was concerned for my family and about how and when it was to happen. What could I possibly say to them that would make them understand? That evening, Kimberly slept through the whole night, the first time she had really been able to sleep deeply since her late husband had died suddenly of a heart attack, three years earlier.

CHAPTER NINE

Home Again, But Not for Long

At the Atlanta airport my return flight to West Palm Beach was delayed and ultimately cancelled due to an equipment problem, and I and dozens of other passengers were redirected to another terminal and another gate for the next flight out. When we arrived at the designated gate, the gate agents were not yet present, and I sat around with some of the other passengers as we waited for the attendants. A man and his wife who were from Stuart recognized me from my commercials and started up a conversation with me. They asked me what it was like to be the Tire King. I told them that even though I was retired now, my life was much like anyone else's except that I was recognized a lot more than most people. They told me that they weren't surprised by this and that they enjoyed my commercials and would really miss seeing them. I thanked them for their kind words. I always appreciated when people enjoyed my spots and felt as if they knew me. As we continued talking, they pointed out a woman who they said had hurt her back badly while carrying her luggage over from the other terminal. I felt compassion for this lady as

I could see she was having difficulty. Within a few minutes the ticket agents arrived and we all got up to get in line for seat assignments. As fate would have it, I wound up in line behind the injured woman.

She was having trouble dragging her bags along, and I offered to help her. She was very grateful and relieved to have the help and, as we chatted in the line, she told me that she had strained her back earlier and that I was a Godsend. Now I had to make a decision. I remembered what Kimberly had taught us in one of the healing classes: *"All spiritual healers must learn discernment. They must learn when to step up and when to sit back"*. I thought about it, reconsidered it, and then finally I overcame my reluctance and I said to her, "I know that this may sound strange, but I feel that I can help your back. If it's okay with you, I would just like to put my hand on it." She replied, "Well if you think it will help, I don't see why not". And as I moved to place my hand on her back, I was guided to exactly the right place, and the energy began flowing just as soon as I touched her. My hands became extremely hot and I could see the change in the way she looked and felt. The stress in her face disappeared, replaced instead with a look of serenity and peace, and I could see the evidence of Spirit moving within her. I knew then that this was no chance encounter. The energy channeled for about ten minutes and then it stopped. It was a really good healing. The pain was completely gone and she was very serene. Afterwards on the plane, she told me that she had a good friend who was into spiritual things, and that she had been meaning to get together with her. Now she said she would, just as soon as she got home. The purpose of spiritual healing is spiritual awakening. Its intention is to open people to a greater understanding of life, of God, and of themselves. Even the Christ worked in this way. His deeds were evidence of a greater Light and a greater power manifesting on earth. I had no doubt that I had been given the privilege of helping this woman to awaken to something more within herself.

After my return home, I continued to focus on my spiritual practice and development. I had no plan other than to take each day one step at a time, and I was beginning to learn that it is the journey itself that has value, and so I was allowing my life to unfold. It was an exciting time for me and also a time of uncertainty. I knew my life was changing and with each day I looked forward to the evidence of Spirit at work. But I also understood that all that I had known, all that I had been was no longer operative, and I would soon be traveling a different road and living a different life. I worried about my children, about my wife, about myself. How could I tell them? How could I tell them what I didn't quite understand myself? What could I say to them that could possibly explain my intention to leave them in favor of some unknown or abstract quest? How could I say it to them in a way they would understand? From that moment when I committed myself to God, I knew my life would change. And now the time was at hand, almost. I spent the next month and a half meditating, reading, learning, studying, and practicing my newfound spiritual skills. I continued to do healings whenever the opportunities occurred, and I was a frequent visitor to the New Age bookstores that were located around town. I knew it was only a matter of time before I would have to make some tough decisions, and I sought out an old friend to ask his advice.

Bill Craddock and I had been friends since we first moved to Florida. We were neighbors at Tanglewood Apartments in Palm Beach Gardens. In 1972, Palm Beach County was a far different place than it is today. There were just over two hundred thousand people in the county then, and the development we see now had barely just begun. It was a time of great opportunity, and many of the pioneers who made their mark here had just arrived. Among our other neighbors at Tanglewood would be two circuit court judges, two state attorneys, the public defender, a number of high priced and high paid lawyers, and a handful of budding businessmen and entrepreneurs, this last group which included Billy and I. We were all very young then, in our twenties, the new pioneers of Atlantis, and we had come to Paradise to start a new life and to make our mark in the world. A number of years after moving out of Tanglewood, Billy divorced his wife. His two boys were sixteen and seventeen then. My youngest son Timmy was sixteen going on seventeen. I wanted to ask Billy how he handled this situation with his own children and if he could give me any guidance.

At the time, I knew intuitively that my son Timmy would take it the hardest. I just had a knowing about this that turned out to be right. My oldest son Jason was twenty-six, and although he could get very emotional about things he considered setbacks, I knew that at the end of the day he would accept and understand my choices. My son Michael was a nineteen year old student and basketball player at the University of Miami, and the prince of the city. Mike was always level-headed, and of all my children, he was the only one who recognized that his parents had never been very happy together. Tim was the youngest and the most vulnerable. He was our baby. Instead of being straight with him, we initially tried to hide what was happening in order to protect his feelings. I wanted to tell him everything, but Jill would hear none of this. But this was not just about me, or Jill, or our children. This was about all of us, about our family, and our futures. The events that had been set in motion would have far reaching and significant effects on all of us. The highest dramas of all are those that are played out on the stage of Spirit, and in the theater of our hearts.

Billy told me exactly what I didn't want to hear, and the thing that I feared the most. Although he shared a close relationship with his older son Mark who had accepted his divorce, his younger son Scott had all but disowned him and their relationship was strained at best. What was I to do? I loved my son Timmy with all of my heart. As a young boy of seven or eight, he would often crawl up onto my lap, wrap his arms around me, and then look into my eyes and smile as he said, "I love you Daddy". Then he would kiss me. My heart would melt each time. I loved him so. But by the time he was a teenager, he had drawn away from me, and would never let me get too close again. In retrospect I know why he did this, although I didn't understand it then. I had shared many previous lives with my children and their mother, and I had spent my current life doing everything I could to provide for them and to protect and insulate them from the difficulties of the world. But now I was to be the instrument of their undoing, and I was sad and worried at the prospect of hurting them. I didn't know how this would come about, or even when. But I knew it would, and that it would be sooner rather than later. And deep within me I knew that somehow we were all part of it, that we had all planned these events at a soul level. And I trusted that everything was in divine order, and that one day we would all know and understand the meaning of all that would transpire, and that we would all be the better for it. At the least this was my hope.

In September I was asked by Gloriana to come down to the Crystal Garden bookstore in Boynton Beach and help her to teach her channeling class. I was happy to do this and I headed there on the night of the class. However, I got the times wrong and I arrived there one hour early. So I spent the time looking around at the books, the merchandise, and at the crystals and jewelry on display. As I was looking at the crystals, the clerk came up to me and asked me if I had ever seen cobaltian calcite. When I replied that I hadn't, she showed me a beautiful drusy pink stone that had just a spot of green malachite in it, which was mounted as a necklace. As I looked at it, immediately it called to me the name "Kimberly". This took me totally by surprise. I hadn't really thought about Kimberly since that day on the road when we said goodbye. Maybe I didn't want to, fearful of where the road would lead. But I knew this necklace was for her, and so I bought it, not really knowing if I would ever give it to her.

The days and weeks passed quickly, and in October I headed back to Delphi to take another round of classes. After flying into Atlanta, I arrived at the school late in the afternoon on the school van with a number of other students. After I settled into my room, I went down to the dining hall for dinner, and then to the main teaching building for evening class. I was the last to arrive. There were a lot of people in this group, some who I knew and others who I didn't. Patricia was there to greet us. And so was Kimberly. They were all gathered around talking and saying hello when I got there. I hugged and greeted the people I knew, all of whom were my former classmates, when suddenly I found myself face to face with Kimberly. I could feel her shyness as she turned away slightly when I looked into her eyes. I noticed that she had cut her hair, something that I would not normally notice, and I told her that I liked it. Then I said hello and we embraced awkwardly. Holy cow, I wasn't prepared for the feelings I felt then. She wasn't either. A surge of energy like an electric current ran between us and I'm sure my legs buckled for a moment. She too felt this as we held on to each other for stability for what seemed an eternity, but was only a few moments. Stunned, we released each other and headed separately into the teaching room where all the others had already taken their seats on the numerous sofas and loveseats there. As chance would have it, there were only two seats left, both next to each other. I took one of the seats. A few seconds later, as if she had been searching for anywhere else to sit, Kimberly took the other.

The feeling between us was electric. I was sure everyone in the room was watching us, and indeed they were. How could they not see the lights and the energy currents moving between us? All of these people were psychic, and many possessed perceptual vision. They couldn't help but see that something unusual and unique was going on. Later some of them asked me what this was. I didn't have an answer for them. Neither did Kimberly. All we knew was that something was up, that the energy between us was undeniable. But what this 'something' was, remained to be discovered. The next evening before class, I went looking for and found Kimberly. I told her that I wanted to speak with her. We spoke for a few minutes. We both agreed that we needed to talk, and we felt it would be better to do so after this class had ended. I was staying for the next class and had a short break in between. So we agreed to get together then. I spent the next week studying in earnest. Although I would have normally had Kimberly as one of my instructors in this class, the group was so large that it had to be split in two, with Kimberly spending most of her time with the other group, resulting in little contact between us.

The end of the class came extremely fast and eternally slow. I had arranged to meet Kimberly at one o'clock in the afternoon on the day class ended. She was waiting for me in front of the school when I arrived. All the other students were gone now. Many of them had sensed something going on between us. One of them warned her not to get involved with me. I didn't know what was in store for us or what I or she would say. We made small talk for a little while and then I told her that I had a gift for her. I gave her the necklace and told her the story about how it called out her name. She loved it and asked me to put it on for her. She related a story to me of how I had come to her in a dream a few weeks earlier, and how we had looked so deeply into each other's eyes. Although she told me she didn't yet understand our connection, she knew that it was significant, that our coming together had been arranged on a cosmic level.

It was a beautiful and sunny Fall day, cool but not cold. We decided to take a walk together on the Healing Passage. The Healing Passage was an area in the adjacent woods through which a fast moving stream passed on its' journey to the river. For thousands of years the Cherokee nation brought their sick bodies and troubled minds here for healing in its therapeutic waters. We walked along the creek, deeper into the woods, and we sat down under one of the giant oak trees that are so abundant here. We stared into each other's eyes for what seemed an eternity, looking deep into one another, into and through the windows of our souls. And like that old fifties song, "Just One Look", just one look was all it took. We both realized and knew in that moment that we had a purpose together: to love, to partner, to grow, to share, to teach, to heal, and to shine God's light out into the world. It was so clear, so beautiful, so true. And when we kissed, there was no doubt about why we had come together and where we were going. Of all the roads I had traveled my entire life; they all had led me here. It was the same for Kimberly, only she had been waiting for me to arrive.

That afternoon, Kimberly related another story to me about our coming together. Some months earlier, her friend Doretta had told her that a man was coming to spend his life with her. Doretta said that he was lacing up his shoes (symbolic for preparing himself) and getting ready to come, and that both he and Kimberly would step in and out of each other's energy, and would not recognize each other at first. The night that Kimberly's Viennese friend Shake (pronounced Shak-kee) had told her that she would meet the man she would be with the rest of her life at Delphi in

August, Kimberly had a vivid dream. She dreamed she was rushing to catch a plane and she was fearful of being late, although the limousine driver assured her that there was plenty of time to make the flight. After what seemed an interminable drive, there parked in the middle of a super highway was a jumbo jet awaiting her arrival. At the plane a man was waiting there to help her get onboard. The only feature she could see of the man was his eyes. That day at the Passage she told me she finally realized whose eyes she had seen in the dream. The eyes belonged to me.

As we headed back to Delphi late that afternoon, I couldn't help but wonder what I was to do now. To say that the attraction between Kimberly and I was great would be a serious understatement. But I wasn't looking to have an affair, nor would I consider it. I had to remain pure and true to myself, and I told Kimberly that. I needed to end it with Jill first before I could give myself to her. She assured me that she understood and that this was also the way she wanted it to be. She said that she was patient and could wait as long as it would take until I got my affairs settled. We both had the knowing that it was our destiny to be to-gether, and that there was nothing that we needed to push or create. It would unfold in its own time and its own way. And so we agreed that this would be the way that we would proceed. I knew inside that one day I would have to go home, break the news to Jill, and do what I had to do. Only after that could we begin our life together. Just the thought of doing this filled me with fear and anxiety.

That night Kimberly and I slept in the same bed together, fully clothed and fully abstinent. Neither of us was prepared for what happened. As we meditated and held hands, a cosmic light show unfolded before our eyes. It went on for hours, parading across our view and our consciousness, every manner of light, symbol, shape, form, and feeling. There were so many things happening, changing, and appearing and parading before us that it was impossible to focus on any of them. What we were seeing was our oneness, and this oneness took and lifted us into a higher state of consciousness. We were looking into the higher mind, the mind of God, and to my simple human mind and perception, much of it was incomprehensible. It was truly universal, a stellar display of fireworks, touched off by the reunion of our two souls, and the joining of our purpose together. It continued for hours as we were mesmerized by it. Finally, at about five in the morning, Kimberly finally said, "Okay Charles, you can stop it now." To which I replied, "Me? I thought you were the one doing it."

The next day my class began, and I spent the remainder of the week going there. The class schedule at Delphi is intensive, and runs morning, afternoon, and evening. I didn't see a lot of Kimberly during the daytime, as she only taught a couple of the classes in the course I was taking. But late at night, after the last class had ended, I would get to see her again. Typically we would meditate together and then fall asleep, arising early the next morning so that I could make it to group meditation, breakfast, and the next class. Later in the week, one of my afternoon classes was interrupted by one of the instructors who called me outside to speak with me. He told me that they had just received a call from my son Jason who said that my Dad had died. I immediately called Jason on the phone, who along with my sister Ro had been attending to my father, and I spoke with them both.

Ro told me that Dad had suddenly taken a turn for the worst that week and had died even before they could finalize the arrangements to place him in hospice care. They both said he had crossed over while in his sleep. He had been having trouble breathing due to the fluid buildup in his lungs, which had to be continually pumped out, and he slept or was unconscious most of the time. She also told me that in his sleep he would call out for his brother Mike, his mother, or others that he had known in life. He would speak with them and laugh, and interact as if they were all together. And in those rare moments when he was awake and was aware of his surroundings, he would ask Ro or Jason what happened to his brother and others who had just been there with him. My father was doing what many people who are near death often do, particularly if they have made previous energetic connections with Spirit. When he was asleep or unconscious, he was traveling to the Astral Plane, the place where most of us go when we die, where he was communing with his loved ones, friends, and relatives on the other side. But because he had not yet died, he was being drawn back to his body, until it was time for him to crossover for good.

I started to make funeral arrangements over the phone, and I asked Jason if he would be able to help coordinate them for me. I told him that I wanted to stay at Delphi, that I thought I could help my father far better from here than I could there. He told me, "Sure Dad, I can handle it." I was very grateful to him for this. My Dad had previously told me that he wanted to be cremated and he wanted me to disburse his ashes in the sea, something I promised I would do. And so I instructed Jason to schedule the cremation to happen in three days, no sooner than that, and also to schedule the funeral service for 11AM Sunday, the day after the cremation. I told him that I was being ordained as a minister this week and would hold the funeral services myself, and that I would fly in to West Palm early Sunday morning. When he asked me why I wanted to wait three days for the cremation, I explained to him that although the physical body dies, the etheric or spiritual life body is still present, and requires three days to withdraw completely.

After I was off the phone, I walked outside to get some air and collect my thoughts. I was sad that my father had died, but I was prepared for it and happy for him, particularly that he was no longer suffering, and because I knew that he was indeed in a better place. He had lived his life in the way he had chosen and, thanks to his illness, he had been given time at the end of it to reflect upon it. He had even asked forgiveness from my mother and had received it, and now he would be celebrated for his journey at the end of his life, by the many loved ones and spiritual friends and beings who awaited his coming. I remembered saying to him one day after a healing, "Dad I want you to know that you have been one of my greatest teachers in this life." Puzzled, he raised his eyebrows, looked at me incredulously and said, "Me? Charles, how could you possibly say that about me?" And I told him, "Dad, if you hadn't done what you did, I doubt that my life would have turned out as it did, and I wouldn't have accomplished all that I have. You have been my great teacher, even though you didn't know it....until now." And then I smiled and hugged him. Sensing his skepticism, I looked him in the eyes and said, "No, really. It's true." He gave me a look which begged to ask if I was sure, and then he smiled and seemed to accept this simple but elusive truth. In his own way, this simple soul had sacrificed a part of his life so that I could fulfill my own. Then he told me he loved me, and I told him I loved him too. My Dad was a simple man. He didn't have much, nor did he need much. But I think the one thing that gave him the most pleasure in his life was that he was proud of me, 'my son' as he used to refer to me whenever he had the chance. Some say that the man who has the most in life is the one who needs the least. That was Stubby.

As I walked along the road, with the cool breeze blowing and the bright sun shining simultaneously in my face, I asked God and the spiritual beings I had come to know to guide and watch over my father. And then it hit me. The realization hit home. I was no longer obligated by my father's karma, and by his father's fathers before him. The debt was paid, the chain broken, and I was free. They call it the 'Sins of the Father', and it refers to a repeated pattern of karmic behavior, generation after generation, which continues on and on until someone finally breaks it. Of my father and his father and his father's father, and God only knows how many Curcios before them, all had abandoned their families, all except me. And even though I was contemplating that very thing now, it wasn't the same. Though one might argue this point, my children were grown and I had provided for my family and their future. This was the truth of it. I also knew that these events had come into their lives for a higher purpose as well. In my heart I wished I could wait one more year until my youngest son Tim finished high school. But I knew that the time was now at hand. And as if to reinforce this point, two of the students from the first class I had ever taken at Delphi, my sisters really, came up to me at that moment and out of the clear blue said, "It's okay Charles. It's okay for you to be free now. Spirit has sent us to tell you this, so you would know."

Three days had now elapsed since my father died, and it was my last day at Delphi on this trip. I would be leaving very early the next morning for my plane to West Palm, in order to arrive in time for the funeral. This particular afternoon, we had gotten out of class early in order to prepare ourselves for the healing sessions that we would perform that evening. My father was on my mind, and I thought I would take the time now to contact him and check to see how he was doing. Unlike what many people believe or fear, there is no Hell per se. There is no unyielding place of eternal damnation, and no heaven or hell result when we die. However, there are seven levels of the Astral Plane, often referred to as the Seven Heavens, where all except the most evolved human beings travel after the death of the temporary personality and the physical body. The lowest level of the Astral Plane, which many compare to the concept of Hell, is the world of unrestrained power and selfish desire. In reality it is more like a purgatorial state, and it is reserved solely for the most incorrigible souls who are so obsessed by their lower passions and desires that they are attracted to and consigned there with others of like demeanor. And because they lack physical bodies with which to enact them, here they are bound, unable to fulfill their desires. Ultimately, these desires die from the lack of fulfillment, and ideally the soul gets another chance on earth. No person who lives a decent life need ever touch this level or even become aware of its existence. The next level of the Astral Plane could be compared to everyday waking consciousness like that which we experience on earth, except for the ability to more quickly manifest our thoughts and intentions. The remaining five levels of the Astral Plane are increasing more heavenly and nirvanic, such that the higher one's state of awareness, the higher the level they occupy.

I found a secluded spot and a comfortable chair down by the river and I felt the peace and serenity that only comes when you are enfolded in the arms of our Earth Mother. I began to breathe rhythmically, focusing only on my breath, feeling it moving into and out of my lungs. As I continued to breathe, I could feel my body relax and my consciousness shift, and I began to lift, as I set my intention to travel to the place where I could be with my father. Moments passed, and then my vision was filled with a brilliant, almost blinding orange light, which I recognized as him. I could feel his presence, the same one I had known throughout my life, and I knew instantly that he was fine. Actually he was far better than that. He was much greater in death than he had ever been in life. No longer the temporary earthly personality of the man they called Stubby, he had reunited with his soul, and he was now the true expression of his True Self. I could feel his burning love for me as I heard him say telepathically, "I love you Charles. Thank you for everything. Please give my love to everyone and let them know not to worry about me." I told him that I would, that I loved him too, and I was very happy to experience him in this way. And then we said goodbye.

After my Father's funeral, I continued with my daily spiritual practice and I made plans to return to Delphi the following month. For the first time I felt unsettled, unsettled about being back on Jupiter Island, and unsettled about where I was going. I was restless and uneasy, and I no longer felt comfortable in my former surroundings. Even the solace I used to feel just walking or riding around my property seemed to escape me now. All bets were off. I continued each day, walking in the light, taking one step at a time.

I returned to Delphi a couple of weeks later. I spoke with Kimberly at length about our life and purpose together. I knew it was right. I knew it was love. I knew that all the roads had led me here. And I knew it was time. At first we expected to take it slowly, but then I told her that I felt strongly that I had to make the move now, or perhaps I never would. Although surprised by this, she understood my feelings and said she would go along with whatever I felt was best. I told her, that after this trip to Palm Beach that I would be returning to Delphi to be with her for good.

CHAPTER TEN

The Hardest Thing

Of all the things I have done in my life, of all the challenges, the setbacks, and the difficulties I have faced, all would pale in comparison to what lay ahead of me now. I knew where I was headed. I knew the road I was to travel. I knew the pain that it would cause. And I knew what I had to do. What had been muddled before was now so very clear, not so much in task but in direction. I wondered how and from where I could find the strength to do it. I was to leave the family that I loved and the life I knew to come to Delphi, for it was here that I would begin my work, my life of service to God. The prospect of telling this to Jill and the boys was overwhelming, and the thought of hurting them was more than I could bear. God, give me the strength, for I know now what I must do.

I had an early evening flight back to West Palm Beach out of Atlanta, and Kimberly drove me there, along with her friend Linda. They were headed to Boca Raton to work, and I was headed home to break the news to Jill. I told Kimberly not to buy a return ticket, that we would be returning to Georgia together. We said goodbye at the security area and went our separate ways to our individual gates. The plane ride home was uneventful. I spent the time meditating, praying, and contemplating how I was going to break the news. I decided that the best way to do it was to just tell it like it was. I shuddered to think what Jill's reaction would be. As we flew down the Martin and then Palm Beach County coastline in preparation for our approach, I was able to see my home on Jupiter Island, and as we continued I took notice of all the landmarks I knew and recognized these past twenty-five years. This had been my home, really the only place I had ever considered in that way, and one I had been sure I would never leave. So many things had happened to me here, where almost everything of meaning in my life had transpired, and I felt sad that now I was going to say goodbye. It was the place where I had raised my family, the place I had found success, and also the place where I found my true purpose. And now I was returning here once more, attempting to detach myself from it, to tell the ones I loved that I was leaving them for good.

Jason picked me up from the airport and drove me home. Jill was grocery shopping, and Mike and Tim were out doing their thing. Jill returned home an hour later. I smiled and said hello to her, and then I hugged her. Memories came flooding back to me. I remembered what she looked like as a young girl when we met. In my mind's eye I saw her in the delivery room and the smiles we shared at the birth of our children. And I remembered all that had come to pass between us. I couldn't help but think what a good woman and mother she was. I felt my compassion for her and my own sense of loss. And although things between us weren't perfect, it was nobody's fault and there was no one to blame. Things were in Divine Order, as they always are, and I asked God to help her, to help our children, and to help me. Then I helped carry the groceries into the house, as I always did when I was home. Inside the house, when she asked me how I was doing, I knew she sensed that something was up. I told her that I was doing fine, that the classes had been great, and that it was nice to be home, which it was. Then I told her that I had something important to talk to her about. When she pressed me to say what, I told her that it could wait, and I suggested that we take a walk on the beach later and talk about it then. She agreed that this would be fine.

A couple of months earlier, on one of my return trips to Delphi, one of the other students from my channeling class, Bella, came running up to me very excited and said that she'd had a dream about me the previous evening which she wanted to tell me about right away. She dreamed that I was in a boat on a river, a river much like the one that runs through Delphi. She said that I had paddled the boat a great distance and it had taken me a long time to get to the place where I was going. She continued to say that I landed the boat on a bank of the river, and that once docked, I worked very hard to clear the land and build a new home, one that was quite beautiful and unique. When I was finished, I surveyed my work, proud and happy with what I had accomplished, and I got back into the boat and paddled back up the river in the direction from where I had come. When I returned, Jill was in the boat with me. I had brought her here to show her what I had created and to share it with her. Jill looked around, shook her head, and refused to stay, despite my entreaties. Instead she got back in the boat, and rowed away by herself, against the current of the river. I remained and continued to build more and more houses.

It was early evening now. The sun was shining, the sky was blue, and there was a nice onshore breeze blowing in our faces, which was typical of November in South Florida after a cold front had passed through on its southerly march down the peninsula, and the wind had resumed blowing out of the southeast once again. The beach was deserted as it always is here and, when we walked over the wooden dune crossover that led to the beach, it was just her, me, and the presence of God which is reflected in everything natural and beautiful here. We sat down on the benches which were built into the dune crossover, and I reached down deep to find the words to begin. One thing I had learned in business that had always helped me to initiate and say something uncomfortable was simply to start the words. My right hand man James 'Sep' Serrabella had taught me that. Just start the words and the rest will follow. As soon as the first word is spoken, the ice will be broken and the words will flow. At Delphi I had learned to breathe first before channeling or saying something important. This time I did both. I took a deep breath, taking in all the energy I could into my lungs, all the strength I could muster, and then I began the words. "Jill", I said, "I'm leaving."

She listened intently for a few moments to what I was saying. And then she said, "What do you mean you're leaving? Where are you going? For how long? When are you coming back?" Here it was, the moment of truth. I considered my answer and then I said, "I'm probably not coming back. I have to go. I must follow my calling." Now she became upset. "What do you mean, you have to follow your calling? You're calling is with me, with your children, with your family. What are you going to say to them?" "The truth", I replied. I told her that she must have seen how much I had been and was changing, and that I had tried my best to let her know everything that was going on, even welcoming her involvement. I said to her that all of these things were real, but that she had never taken them seriously or me. I explained that my entire life had been leading up to this point, and that now I must follow the road wherever it leads me. I told her that we had come together for a purpose in this life, and now that purpose was complete. I no longer resented her and she could no longer control me. I went on to say that, even though she wouldn't understand what I was saying until a later time in her life, she had played her role perfectly. She had done everything right, everything she had agreed to do, everything I had asked of her, all that she had asked of herself.

Jill then said to me that she didn't understand any of this, that she wasn't playing any role, and that she didn't understand what I was trying to say. And then she said, "How could you do this? How could you do this to your children, to our family, to me?" And then she began to cry, something she never did in front of me, something she swore she would never do again in front of any man ever since the day her father left their home when she was eleven. I said, "Jilly, please don't' cry. This is not your fault. This is not something you can control. Nor can I. This is something I must do." And she said again, "How could you do this to me? I wouldn't do this to you." And like an arrow it penetrated my heart, for I never dreamed I could do this to her either. And, as if I was fortified by Spirit in that very moment, the words came through me, "Yes you would. You would if you were in my place."

Jill and I decided that we would tell the children together. I wanted to meet with them privately, but she insisted that she be there too. She also wanted to exclude Timmy, preferring not to cause him any pain. I told her that I thought this was a bad idea, that he was a bright kid who had the right to know. But I acquiesced to what she wanted, at least for time being. So I told Jason and Mike who, although not very happy about it, accepted it as something I strongly wanted to do, particularly after they tried to convince me otherwise and saw that I wasn't budging. We kept Tim in the dark, although I told him later what I was doing. We were all headed to Miami that evening to watch Michael's basketball team celebrate opening night. Mike played for the University of Miami. Each year, at the beginning of basketball season, they would hold a big event where they would scrimmage other teams, showcase their talent, and kick off the start of the season. Jill and I drove separate cars down to Miami that night. I had already packed the things I wanted to take with me back to McCaysville and loaded them into my car. My plan was to pick up Kimberly in Ft. Lauderdale and make the drive back to Georgia together the next day. I just couldn't spend another night at home. If I were going to get this done, I knew I couldn't prolong it.

After the night's events were over, I was standing outside

THE HARDEST THING « 101

in the parking lot with Tim and Jason, while Jill was waiting for Mike to come out of the locker room. I decided to pull Tim off to the side and explain things to him. He already knew that something was up because of the strange way we were all acting. And in the best and simplest way I could present it to him, I told him about my life and how things were changing for me, and about how I now had to move on to do something that was really important. And just like I had done with his brothers, I told him that I had a calling from God which I had to follow. I hadn't yet told any of them about Kimberly. He asked, "Does that mean you're leaving us, for good?" I said, "Tim, I love you. You know that. No matter where this journey leads me, I will always love you and keep you in my heart. When I'm not with you, I'll carry you with me, and I'll come to visit you as often as I can." He thought about it for a moment and said, "I don't think it's very nice for you to hurt Mom like this." In my heart I knew he was speaking for his Mother and for himself. "I know Tim," I said, "This is hard for me too." The last thing I ever wanted to do, or would ever remotely consider, was to hurt my children.

After the basketball event we all drove to Coconut Grove to have dinner. I drove my car by myself, and Jill, her mother, and my three boys were in hers. They knew that my plan was to leave afterwards. It would be the last time in a very long time that I would have dinner with my family. I don't know where I found the strength, except I knew that it came from somewhere within me. For the first time ever, we all felt a little uncomfortable together. Normally we would laugh and joke and have fun, but on this night we were all pretty solemn. We were seated outside in one of those many restaurants here that have tables and chairs setup on the sidewalk. Normally this would be one of the best seats in the house for viewing the showcase of glamorous and unusual people who turned out each night to dine, shop, walk the streets, and party. But on this evening we were little interested in the activity on the street. Seated right next to me was a psychic reader who was doing Tarot readings for ten dollars. I was feeling sure in my convictions but unsure in my actions. So I asked her to give me a reading, hopeful that she would confirm what I was doing. When the reader started to ask me questions, my mother-in-law blurted out, "Did he tell you that he's leaving his family?" That kind of broke the energy, and I thanked the reader and paid her, surprised at myself for not trusting what I already knew.

After dinner we walked a bit. Jill was mostly silent except for a sarcastic word or two she sent my way. I was surprised she wasn't angrier, and I think the realization hadn't hit home yet. But I understood how she must have felt. Betrayed, overwhelmed, shocked, surprised, but maybe not really surprised, and hurt were just some of the things I sensed she was feeling. And the boys seemed puzzled and confused. I told my children, "Boys, I may be leaving here, but I'm not leaving you. I swear." That seemed to help, but not a lot. We made our way to the parking garage, and before you knew it, we were standing at my car. Theirs was parked about a dozen spaces away. I embraced each of my children and told them I loved them, and then I attempted to hug Jill, but all she would let me do was to kiss her briefly on the cheek. And then I got in my car and drove away. I watched them watch me in shock and disbelief, and as I turned the corner, they began to cry. It all happened so quickly, so suddenly. And then I was gone.

On my way up Interstate 95 I was in a daze. I was distraught and relieved, all at the same time. I began to question myself, my actions, my motives. I called upon God for re-assurance, and even though I could feel his presence, I felt totally alone. Am I doing the right thing? Is this what He really wants me to do? Is this truly my purpose? Or am I still the victim of my own pride, and the instrument of my own ego? I began to weep. I began to wail. All my life I had always protected my family. I had always done my best to keep them free from harm, from pain, from anything that could hurt them. And now I had become the instrument of their undoing. I cried out, "Oh God please help me, help me to be the servant of your will." And that small still voice within me said ever so softly, "Remember who you are and why you've come here. This is for their growth as well as yours."

A sense of calm now filled me. But I was still concerned for them and I asked God for His help. I drove to Boca Raton very late that night and took a room in the hotel where Kimberly and Linda were staying. In the morning Kimberly and I would be driving back to North Georgia together, while Linda would be remaining in Ft Lauderdale. Well here I was. I had made the break, and was headed for my new life. It was the most difficult and painful thing I ever did, and for years I would often feel the energies of guilt and regret gnawing at me. But I knew within myself that my ac-tions were consistent with my Higher Self's and God's plan for me. What remained to be seen was if I could complete what I had now begun. And I also knew that in the future I would now be able to give my children gifts like unconditional love, wisdom, insight, guidance, compassion, and sensitivity, things which I was unable to give them before, and gifts that no amount of money in the world can buy.

I made one more significant trip back to the place I called home, back to Jupiter Island, a place I never thought I'd ever leave, to see my family to whom I had devoted my life, and who I would never consider hurting, even in my wildest dreams. My youngest son Timmy was not around much during this time. Although he was off on a trip with some of his friends, I think he stayed away purposely so that he wouldn't have to see me. Tim was angry and hurt, and he felt betrayed. I missed him more that I can express. When he was a young boy, I felt and experienced his love. Now he acted like he hated me. Once when I went to his school to pull him aside and talk to him, he didn't want to see or acknowledge me at all. Finally when I cornered him he said, "Dad, I don't know what happened. I had just turned sixteen, I had a new car, I was on top of the world, and then you left. You made your decision and that's that!" Nothing I could say or do would soften his heart. Fortunately, I knew that in time we would come together again. Two different psychics had told me so. But it was hard going for me, also for the boys, and of course for Jill. But I knew in my heart that we would all be the better for it. I trusted in God that it was so.

The week I spent here passed very quickly, although I think I never enjoyed my little piece of paradise as much as I did on this trip. During the week I spent a lot of time with my sons Jason and Mike. We talked, hung out, went out to eat, and spent as much time together as we could. I felt closer to them now than I ever had before. I found myself speaking with them as a friend, and taking the time to listen to them, something I hadn't done very well in the past. I was always preoccupied with my own stuff and my own needs then, and I realized that one of the best things I had to give them now was the one thing I hadn't given them very much of before, and that was myself. They both took the opportunity, independent of each other, to make a final run at me, asking me if I was sure that I knew what I was doing. I think inside they hoped that this was another of my new distractions, where I would run headlong into something new and then, after I had mastered it sufficiently, finally tire of it. But I knew that they now realized that this was different, and there was no turning back. I assured them that God had a plan for me, and even though none of us might see it fully now, that in time we would all know the truth of it.

On my last day there, Jill returned from her trip. But she decided to take a hotel room that evening, and then return to the house the next day after I had gone. That night she called to talk with me. We talked about the boys, our lives, and about nothing. She asked me if I really had to go. "Why couldn't you stay" she asked "with me and the boys, with your family?" I could hear her sobbing gently as she waited for my answer. I tried to think of the right words to say, the words that could make her understand, something to comfort her and make her feel better. "Jilly", I began, "I want you to know that if there was any way I could, I would. Believe me, the last thing I wanted to do was to hurt you and the children, or to break apart our family. But this thing is bigger than me, or us. You were there when it began. You know what happened. I have to follow my heart wherever it leads me. I hope that one day you'll understand." "I don't understand anything", she said, "except that you're leaving, and I can't do anything about it". "Oh honey", I said, "Understand this, that I love you and appreciate everything you've ever done for me and for our children. I promise you that one day you'll know and see everything clearly. I promise". And she said simply, "I have to go now. Goodbye Charles." "Goodbye Jill", I said, "Take care of yourself." I asked God to watch over her and my children. In June of 1998 our divorce became final.

Afterwards I went over to the main house to say goodbye to Jason and Michael. "Dad, we love you", said Jason. "Are you sure you have to go?", asked Mike, the look of hope still in his eyes. And I replied, "Look boys. Even though I'm going I'm not leaving you. You are my sons and I love you dearly. No matter where this path of mine leads me, I will always love you and keep you in my heart. And I will come to visit you often." Then I asked both of them to smile for me, something I would often do when they were growing up. They both did their best to give me their best smile. And then we hugged and kissed each other and said goodbye. They stayed in the house as I got into my car. As I began to drive away I stopped to watch them both in an embrace, crying and comforting each other. The expression of love between them, in the middle of their sorrow, was one of the most beautiful things I have ever seen. I thanked God for the experience, as I realized that some good things had already begun. Jason and Mike had never been very close or even friendly when they were growing up. Yet here they were, consoling each other, two brothers sharing their love and their care for each other, perhaps for the very first time.

There is a common misconception in Christianity as to what the Christ (whose true name was Yahoshua) actually said while hanging on the cross. The phrase, "Eli, Eli, lama sabachtani", is generally accepted as one of the last things spoken by him, and which translates as, "My God, my God, why have you forsaken me?" But the truth is that, although these words are essentially accurate, there is a single syllable missing which changes the meaning entirely. What the Christ really said was, "Eli, Eli, lama asabachtani" which means, "My God, my God, why have I forsaken you?" When that moment of truth comes for you, what will you say? What will you choose?

CHAPTER ELEVEN

Kimberly

The first time I saw her she came gliding into the main teaching room. Her feet made no sound and her long flowing dress and long blond hair seemed to be powered by the wind. She flowed into the room effortlessly, and when she spoke her accent was difficult for me to discern. At first I thought it was German, but soon realized it wasn't. She appeared very youthful, younger than her years or history would suggest, and very self-confident, like she knew things that we didn't, that she was here now to teach us. She was like a goddess, come to earth to fulfill her mission, and to instruct the rest of us about God and Spirit and ourselves. There was also an air of mystery about her that was quite intriguing. What was her story? What was she doing here, in this remote and far off place? Her name was Kimberly Hayes Panisset, daughter of Patricia Hayes, and widow of the famous Brazilian healer, Mauricio Panisset, the Man of Light. She is also the author of the book, Man of Light, which chronicles her life with Mauricio and the incredible gifts of light that were quite visible and dramatic, which would emanate and flash out from his body and bring healing to others.

Kimberly has been in spiritual work her entire life. The oldest of five children her mother had birthed with her husband Harry Hayes by the age of 24, Kimberly was a spiritual pioneer since the time she could walk and talk. Her mother Patricia had been administrative assistant to the psychic Arthur Ford until his death, and Patricia spent all her time developing spiritual training techniques in areas like intuition, energy use and perception, healing, meditation, and numerous other ways of connecting with, expressing, and accessing the power of Spirit. Both Arthur Ford and Patricia Hayes were deeply involved with Spiritual Frontiers Fellowship, which was founded by Arthur in 1956. Their mission was and is to be "an interfaith, non-profit movement" of religious leaders, writers, and business and professional persons who feel a kinship with and have a concern for the growing Western interest in altered states of consciousness and mystical experiences.

Since Patricia was a young mother saddled with 5 children, her children would be the subjects through whom she would test and teach her spiritual techniques. And so from an early age Kimberly was developing the skills, expertise, and knowledge of God and Spirit, and practical ways she could use and bring through the love and wisdom of God and share it with others. All of her brothers and sisters became quite adept at developing and expressing their spiritual gifts and abilities. Being the oldest and spiritually most capable of the group of five children, Kimberly became the leader and focal point for the group. Kimberly has spent a large part of her life assisting Patricia in bringing through and developing the spiritual techniques and subjects being taught at Delphi University today. I remember a story she told me once, starting when she was eight years old, about how she always liked to hide behind the curtains and watch Arthur trance channel. Once she watched as he did this for the Queen of England, who was there decked out in her royal robes. Arthur was like a grandfather to Patricia's children who often spent time at his home. Other visitors she encountered there were Bishop Sheen, Ruth Montgomery, and astronaut Edgar Mitchell.

Like her mother Patricia Hayes before her, Kimberly was gifted with incredible psychic and spiritual abilities which she developed from the time she was a little girl. She has the gift of auric vision, which means she can see people's auras. The human auric field is the combination of energy emanations that radiate from the physical and from the subtle bodies: etheric, emotional, and mental. Activity by or any changes in the thoughts, feelings, and emanations of these bodies creates changes of color within the auric field. Kimberly can "read" a person's aura, something she thought as a child that everyone could do. If a person told a lie, she would know it by the color changes in their auric field. If they were angry, shades of crimson would emanate. A spiritually aware person radiates beautiful blues, violets, and yellow in their aura, a selfish person shades of brown and red, a fearful person shades of gray, and a deceitful person gray and green.

Kimberly is the best psychic reader I know. She is such a clear channel that she can take one look into a person's eyes and know that person's whole story. Sometimes I feel she can read my mind, which makes for a very interesting relationship between us. Sometimes I can read hers, but not as regularly. At an early age Kimberly tired of people discounting her because of her young years and patronizing her about growing up to be 'just like her mother'. And, although she was destined to do spiritual work and was always dedicated to her spiritual mission, she temporarily left her spiritual practice to go out into the world to find herself. She has lived in Calgary and Vancouver, Canada, in Southern California in Irvine, and of course in North Carolina and Georgia at Delphi University where she has both studied as a student and served on staff as an instructor. At Delphi in 1990, she would meet the man who would have a profound impact on her and her life, Mauricio Panisset, the Man of Light.

Chronicled by Shirley MacLaine in her book Going Within, by Dr. Wayne Dyer in his book Modern Magic, and by Kimberly in her book Man of Light, Mauricio possessed a rare gift, the gift of light phenomena. Bright lights could be physically seen flashing like lightning, coming from various parts of his body when he did his healing work. These flashes of blue, white, and other colored lights were beyond human comprehension and would emanate from his hands, his heart, third eye, and from and around other parts of his body whenever he invoked them to work. Mauricio used these lights to miraculously heal the sick and the dying, and to open others to a greater awareness of God and themselves. The purpose of all phenomena and miracles is to open people to greater possibility, to the possibility that God does indeed exist, and that he works through ordinary people like you and me. Dr. Wayne Dyer wrote about

Mauricio, "When I first walked into a room with him I immediately felt that he was radiating an extremely high energy from his body. He literally glowed with the high energy of light and love. Upon meeting him I was immediately placed at ease and I felt as if I were in the company of someone who could actually touch my soul". Almost thirty years her senior, people couldn't understand how the relationship between Kimberly and Mauricio was going to work. The difference in their ages attracted almost as much notoriety as did the healing lights that emanated from and through Mauricio. But theirs was a great love that transcended age and time.

Kimberly and Mauricio alternated their time between the United States and Brazil, where they opened an orphanage for children in the wilderness about seventy miles from Brasília. There their life was hard and Kimberly became a regular "Brasilera", learning the Portuguese language, raising her two children, Marshall and Patrick, and providing basic needs for her family and the orphaned children in their care. They had no electricity, plumbing, or running water, but they did have a generator and a well which provided for their basic needs. Kimberly and Mauricio shared a love that was timeless and ageless. As Mauricio said when he met Kimberly for the first time in this life: "I've been searching for you for 400 years". Mauricio died suddenly of a heart attack in 1993, after spending but a few years together with Kimberly. And although she tried to continue their work there, her time in Brazil was finished, and she returned to the United States and assumed her full time role as a director and instructor for Delphi University.

Today Kimberly continues Mauricio's healing ministry and teaches the process of Light Energization™ to students of healing here at Delphi. During their time together, Kimberly served as Mauricio's apprentice, and she is the one who formalized and developed the techniques that she teaches today. Light Energization™ is far more than physical healing. It is a sacred process that raises the Kundalini, the main spiritual energy circuit in the body, up through the chakras and opens spiritual gateways which allows one to connect with higher levels of cosmic and divine intelligence, as well as one's own Higher Self. Through this connection, spiritual vision opens, communication with higher realms becomes possible, and one can access their higher spiritual abilities. A mystical experience often occurs. The purpose of all spiritual healing and phenomena is spiritual awakening. There are miracles happening every day in our world. One simply has to pay attention, and be open to receive and believe in them.

Of all the roads I have traveled, of all that I have learned, from our very first moments together, my love Kimberly has been my greatest teacher and friend. Through her I have learned so much. I have learned about energy and how it works. I have learned about love and about God. I have learned to be a better healer and a better channel of God's love, light, and healing. And I have learned so much about myself and about existence from this simple, complicated, beautiful, and loving spiritual master, that my words don't do her justice. She is my love and my life, and I never really knew love until I found it with her. We also have karmic lessons together that aren't always pleasant or comfortable, as sometimes we help each other by setting up the negatives from which we both learn. We are soul mates who have come together now as we have before, to fulfill our spiritual purpose and also to help each other heal and grow as spiritual beings trying to be human. Kimberly has not only taught me about God and the workings of Spirit, or of healing and how to be better at doing it, but also about the true meaning of love and how to express it. And she has unselfishly sacrificed herself to my own failings so that I could learn and grow and develop what we all must learn to do. The evolution of love is to grow from selfishness to selflessness, to evolve from taking into giving. This is what the Christ tried to teach us, and where man has so often failed himself.

CHAPTER TWELVE

Egypt

In July of 1996, just before coming to Delphi, I signed up for a spiritual journey to Egypt that was to occur the following January, a trip that never materialized. I knew that something significant awaited me in Egypt. I just wasn't sure what it would be. At the age of five I had the nightmares. I dreamed I was in a pit in Egypt, covered by snakes, vipers, and asps of all different types and sizes. Unlike most dreams, I was unable to shake it. Regardless of whether I was asleep or awake, and despite the love and care of my mother who had come rushing to my aid and stayed with me the entire time, I was overwhelmed and terrified by these slithering creatures and my predicament. Even when I was awake they were present, and the experience was just as real as it must have been then. The nightmare persisted for three whole days.

I have experienced many past lifetimes in Egypt. Once I was chief advisor to Pharaoh, successfully serving him and his son after him. And even though I had the ultimate power, I lived a solitary existence, often yearning for a life of simplicity with the common people. I would often find myself alone in the palace, listening to them celebrate their simple existence in song and dance, and being overcome with the feelings of loss and envy. On another occasion, when I was thirteen years old, I was one of the twelve initiates of the priesthood in the Temple of Rah, the highest order in all of Egypt. When I spoke out against the practice of human sacrifice as an offering to God for greater crop yields, I myself became the offering. And even though they were kind enough to drug me beforehand, I could still feel them cutting out my heart, even though the pain was not so great. On another occasion I made handwritten copies of the holy books and sacred prayers and incantations, for I felt that they belonged to all of the people, and not just the priests. For that I was forced to flee for my life, and I lived in exile deep in the Valley of the Nile, a hermetic existence of prayer and meditation alone with God, which frankly wasn't all that bad. And although I have never tried to revisit it, I'm sure that the lifetime which ended in the snake pit was perhaps the least pleasant of them all.

Kimberly and I had planned to go to India in December of 1996 with her parents Patricia and Marshall. But Marshall became ill and could not go. So Kimberly and I decided to go to Egypt instead. We planned to stay in Giza the whole time, the home of the Sphinx and the Great Pyramid, and possibly arrange a side trip to the mountain of Moses, Mt. Sinai, if it was practical. It would be an opportunity for Kimberly and I to get to know each other better and to more fully discover and develop our spiritual connection. I knew deep down that this trip was important for many reasons, and I was looking forward to it, despite any reservations I may have had. We arrived in Cairo late at night, cleared customs, and took a taxi to our hotel which was directly next to the pyramids. It was a very overcast evening and the visibility was so poor that we couldn't see anything at all.

The next morning we awoke, and there, directly outside our window stood the Great Pyramid. The sight of it was overwhelming. A flood of memories came rushing back to me and I became very excited at the prospect of going there. We decided to have breakfast first and then to go over afterwards. The land surrounding the pyramids here used to be lush, green, and fertile. But now it is just a desert. One had to walk about a mile up a barren hillside to get there from the main entrance. Along the way are hundreds of camel jockeys, street vendors, beggars, and solicitors of every kind. Having been here before, Kimberly advised me not to acknowledge or engage with any of them. For if I did, she warned, I would regret it, and they would never leave us alone. So we walked to the Great Pyramid but decided not to go in because of the long lines of people that had already formed. Instead we chose to walk over to the two other pyramids, although it's commonly understood that the two smaller pyramids (not that they're small by any standard) do not have the energy or the significance of the Great Pyramid.

The Great Pyramid is a marvel of architecture, the last of the remaining Seven Wonders of the World. The precision with which it is built and the uniformity of its construction could not be duplicated today. History teaches us that it is approximately four to six thousand years old and was constructed by the Pharaoh Cheops upon the hard work and broken backs of Hebrew slaves. The closest location from which the mammoth 70 ton blocks of granite used to protect the King's Chamber could be found was near the city of Syene, about five hundred miles down the Nile River. Conventional wisdom has it that the huge stones used in the construction of the pyramid were mined, fashioned, transported by land, and then floated great distances down the Nile on reed barges. Once they arrived near Giza, they were then unloaded and then transported by wagon to the pyramid building site. This and other accepted theories about how the Pyramids were built are fairy tales. Spiritual wisdom tells us that the first stone 'laid' was the capstone, and it and all the other stones were levitated into place from the top down and the bottom up.

Despite its mammoth size and dimensions, the Great Pyramid contains just three small chambers. It is not a tomb, nor does its construction lend itself to any practical human use, except one. Although the two upper chambers were later named by Muslims according to the shape of their roofs, the third or subterranean chamber has no modern name. Because of its flat roof, the upper chamber is called the King's Chamber, and the middle chamber with its rounded roof is known as the Queen's Chamber. The lower chamber is known to some people today as "The Pit", for reasons which will become clear.

There is an ancient inscription within the Great Pyramid which indicates that it was built when the star Lyra was in the Constellation of Cancer, about 73,000 years ago. Hebrew cosmology states that Enoch of biblical fame, also known as the Great Atlantean Initiate Thoth or the Greek god and messenger Hermes Trimegistus, built the great pyramid in anticipation of the Great Flood in order to protect the scientific and esoteric knowledge of the day. So why then do the Egyptian archeologists maintain, and the scientific communities accept the notion that the pyramids are only a few thousand years old?

On a particularly slow morning I questioned the Chief Guide about this. After I asked my questions, he looked around to make sure no one was within earshot, and then he said with a wink, a smile, and a shrug of his shoulders: "The Prophet (Mohammed) says that God created the world six thousand years ago. Who am I to argue with the Prophet?" Kimberly and I both got a chuckle out of that.

The truth is that the Great Pyramid serves and has served two purposes, both of which are spiritual in nature. First, the Great Pyramid is really a cosmic transceiver which receives the cosmic light transmissions from the constellations of Pleiades and Orion, and then redistributes these life force energies to the rest of the earth through twelve individual light stations located around the planet. Second, the Great Pyramid is also an initiation chamber. In ancient times, and now once again in modern times, the initiate who was ready to enter into a life of service to God took their initiation in the Great Pyramid. The list of initiates will surprise you. Moses was initiated there. So was Jesus. So too were Plato, Socrates, and Aristotle. Alexander the Great took his initiation there as did Julius Caesar, the Pontifus Maximus of Rome. Throughout time many great men and woman, and many others great but unknown were initiated in the

Great Pyramid. The graduates of the mystery schools of old, those ancient and sacred institutions of Egypt, Greece, India, Tibet, and other places, who preserved the spiritual truths through time and turmoil, worked and studied and braved sometimes severe tests and challenges so that they could receive their initiation in the Great Pyramid. It was the culmination of many years of hard work and thinning ranks for the attainment and privilege of initiation. A successful initiation resulted in the highest spiritual powers of the initiate becoming activated through the light energies of the Pyramid. Sometimes the initiate never made it past the first chamber.

The lower chamber of the Great Pyramid was known in ancient times as the Chamber of Trial. To access this place, one has to enter the Great Pyramid and then descend hundreds of feet downward through a pitch black tunnel, about four feet square, that leads one down to the chamber, which lies far below ground level. And although there are two sarcophagi there in the chamber purportedly for the initiate to lie in, he must first use his own wits and intuition to discover that the true place of initiation lies behind a secret door hidden in one of the walls. It is there he must lie and wrestle with his own shadows, and face the lower energies that lie within his energy fields and which for the most part he has created himself or has invited to come in.

At the turn of the nineteenth century, the Great Pyramid at Giza was opened to the public. Within days the first visitor died in the lower chamber, followed by dozens more in the months and years to come. Thus, the legend of the Curse of the Pharaohs was born. Within a few years this chamber was ruled off limits, and is still closed to the public today. The only way this place is now accessible is with an official archeological tour or by special permit which must be purchased from the Egyptian Bureau of Antiquities. Because of its uniqueness as a cosmic receiver and its specialized construction, certain of the light energies that enter the Great Pyramid are segregated and distributed to the individual chambers.

In the Chamber of Trial the feminine black light energy spiral is directed. This energy is an aspect of the Holy Spirit, or the feminine creative aspect of the Godhead. It is this Divine Feminine energy that manifests form in the physical world and gives birth to creation, and it is this energy each of us uses to create our lives, even though most people are unaware of its form or function. Because of the influx and concentration of feminine energy inside the Chamber of Trial, fourth dimensional space is created there. Many believe the Fourth Dimension to be the realm of time travel. But in reality, it is the realm of instantaneous thought arrangement and manifestation. The initiate entering the lower chamber would become more and more afraid as he descended deeper into the darkness. And these fears would ultimately manifest right before his eyes. Because he knew what was in store for him and was prepared to face his fears, he was able to overcome them and gain the insight that fear and our lower nature or shadows are here to teach us. That is unless he succumbed to them, in which case he would not complete his initiation. Contemporary visitors on the other hand, had no such preparation or forewarning. When they entered the lower chamber of the pyramid, they manifested and had to face their own worst nightmares, and for some, they were killed by the fear of them.

A successful initiate, male or female alike, who completed the Chamber of Trial would then be guided to the highest chamber, the Chamber of Awareness or King's Chamber as it is known today. Here he would lie in the sarcophagus as the masculine or white light spiral would enter the initiate's third eye and activate the pineal gland which lies directly in the middle of the brain. Formerly the size of a walnut, this gland has atrophied in modern man to the size of a pea. This ductless gland is the key to psychic vision and spiritual perception. The initiate would lie there in a death-like state for three days as his spirit, freed from the trappings of the physical body, wandered the universe in his Ka or spiritual state, where he recognized and experienced the truth of who he is and in so doing achieved true enlightenment or self-awareness. And because he could leave and enter his body at will, he attained true immortality while still living in a body, and he knew without a doubt who and what he really was. After the initiation was concluded, the initiate moved to the central chamber, the Chamber of Harmony (now called the Queen's Chamber) where he was revived, fed, and where he received balance and grounding before re-entering the physical world once more. Only now the initiate was different, much different, and ready to take on a new role and a new way of life.

Kimberly and I spent the next week meditating, shopping, eating at our friend Samir's restaurant, which was only a stone's throw away from our hotel, and visiting other sacred sites in and around Giza. Because we wanted to be initiated ourselves and follow the initiatory steps, we needed access to all of the chambers of the Great Pyramid, including the ability to lie inside the sarcophagus of the King's Chamber without distraction or interruption. Samir suggested that we purchase a permit which would give us private and exclusive access to the Great Pyramid for a period of four hours which could be 6pm to 10Ppm, 10pm to 2am, or 2am to 6pm. We opted for 10 to 2. Samir's man drove us to downtown Cairo and to the antiquities office where we were able to obtain the permit for two thousand Egyptian pounds, about six hundred dollars. Two days later came the big day.

That evening we prepared ourselves with prayer and meditation. We bathed in frankincense which we bought from one of the many perfume oil vendors that abound in Giza. This vendor was a spiritual man and also a cousin of Samir. Flower oils have been cultivated and processed in the Nile River Valley for as long as man has occupied this place, and it is still the source for most of the world's perfumes and fragrances. We were very excited and full of anticipation that evening as Samir picked us up at the hotel to drive us directly to the entrance of the Great Pyramid. There we were met by a handsome, polite, and clean cut young man from the Bureau of Antiquities, who explained what we could expect. He told us that we would be on our own in the pyramid, but that there would be guards outside to help us should the occasion arise. But he advised us that since sound did not travel very well inside the pyramid, we should try to make our own way out before calling for help. When he asked us if we wanted to keep the few lights that were inside the pyramid turned on, we told him to give us about twenty minutes to reach the lower chamber and then turn them off. He said he would do so and that when it was time he would turn the lights back on, although from inside we would see them only dimly, if at all. We thanked him and said goodbye and then we began our descent into the lower chamber. We decided to divide our time up equally in the three chambers, approximately sixty minutes each plus twenty minutes for travel. We were equipped with water, flashlights, candles, and a large bag of crystals and minerals that I wanted to charge in the sarcophagus of the King's Chamber. As we descended lower and lower into the "pit", I was very conscious of keeping my thoughts high and my feelings clear and pure. I felt like Dan Akroyd in the movie Ghostbusters, concerned that my thoughts might conjure up the StaPuff Marshmallow Man Monster or something like that.

I had never felt so enlivened in my life as I did here as we descended into the depths of the pyramid. We made our way slowly down the tunnel and arrived at the Chamber of Trial. We found the opening, lit a candle, and laid down to meditate and to ask for what we needed, consistent with our highest good. As if on cue, the moment we joined hands the lights went out. We were not afraid nor was there reason to be. We had come here to receive God's gifts of love and light, to affirm our connection to All That Is, and to experience this unique and marvelous place. Almost at once our vision expanded, and we could see both the earth plane and the higher dimensions as well. We could move effortlessly between worlds and although it wasn't laid out before us, we both saw and knew the future and our purpose. We had come together not by accident, but with a plan. And much like the ancient mysteries schools, our role was to teach others, to serve as healers both for them and for ourselves, and to continue the work at Delphi. Our mission was to provide the place and to build and expand it, a place where people could come together to discover their spiritual gifts, to heal and empower themselves, and then to help others do the same. Best of all, we knew that this was also God's purpose for us, and that God would support us in our work.

As we made our way up to the King's Chamber, the higher we climbed the higher we felt. I now knew what it meant to feel the power of the Holy Spirit within me, and the forty or so pounds of crystals, water, and other stuff I was lugging around seemed weightless. Kimberly waited patiently as I prepared to take my place in the sarcophagus. I carefully placed the crystals around the interior walls and I laid down between them. The feeling was electric. At this time I had fairly long hair, and as soon as I felt the energy, my hair stood on end, just like it does on those electricity generating machines so popular in science institutes. I actually felt and could sense the ones that had laid here before me, and I was at once ecstatic and humbled by the thought of it. I could feel the light spiral entering my forehead and some pressure in my third eye and within my brain. I also realized at that moment that the initiations that had taken place here were from a bygone era, and that modern man was now tasked and blessed in other ways to discover the truth of his existence. But nonetheless, here we were and it was awesome.

Time passed quickly as a parade of symbols and objects passed across my vision. When I asked for a meaningful sign, an altar appeared that was surrounded in cosmic blue light. The altar was flat on top and it was wider at the base than at the top, sort of like a triangle with the top taken off. Above the altar was a crescent moon, a magic moon, lighted not on the side or top, but upon the bottom. At once I recognized this as a symbol of spiritual magic, and I realized that it was showing me that my own state of enlightenment had begun. What had been previously dark (my own awareness) had now magically begun to shine its light and uncover its true nature, although the greater part of this light was still obscured, just as the crescent moon I was viewing. And as if to confirm this, I involuntarily opened my eyes and much to my amazement I still saw the altar, the moon, and the light in exactly the same way I had seen it with my eyes closed. I spent the next few minutes opening and closing my eyes and marveling at the wonder of it all. Then I became disoriented, and I couldn't tell whether my eyes were open or closed unless I touched them physically. Only when I wanted it to, did the vision finally disappear.

After Kimberly's experience in the sarcophagus, we made our way to the Queen's Chamber and found ourselves being balanced and grounded. Soon after, the lights came on and we left the Great Pyramid. After tipping the lineup of guards who miraculously appeared at the entrance when we were leaving, we made our way back to our hotel, knowing full well that the experience had touched us on many levels. The next evening, our last in Egypt, we had dinner and then returned to our room. It was a beautiful clear night, and about 3am we went out onto the balcony to view the Great Pyramid one last time. We were hardly prepared for what we saw. There before our eyes was a vast array of what I can only call lightships: hovering, flying to and fro', and entering and leaving the space around the pyramid. There were large ones, small ones, ships in V-shaped formations, and ships of all shapes and configurations, flying singular and in groups. It was an intergalactic light show and it confirmed to us that there is more in the universe than meets the eye, much more. For certain there was a great deal of activity going on, in and around the Great Pyramid, which I'm sure few people knew about or sensed. And we both knew that we were part of a great order and a great plan, and that many of our cosmic brothers and sisters had come here as well.

CHAPTER THIRTEEN

Signs & Wonders

One day as I sat in the Sun with my naked back facing it, I set my intentions to breath in the Christ energies, energies which many believe emanate from the Sun. I focused on breathing the Sun's rays into my heart, and I could feel the energies entering my body. That evening when I looked into the mirror, there was a perfect white circle extending around the back of my heart chakra, about seven inches in diameter, the evidence of my earlier encounter. By this time I was getting used to unusual phenomena and stories about it. But it was nothing compared to what I would experience later on. Hanging out with Kimberly, one could not avoid this phenomena if they tried.

My first encounter with spiritual phenomena occurred many years earlier, in December, 1984. It was the day before trial in Federal Court in Miami, where I was locked in a legal battle with one of my competitors. We were winning in the marketplace and the competitor had fabricated a federal lawsuit in an attempt to overwhelm and stop us from entering their home market in Miami. It was the eve of trial, and my lawyers and employees were sure I was on the verge of a nervous breakdown. Maybe I was. I was running around the law offices barking orders, walking on the ceiling, wondering and worried about what else we should do to be prepared. I was an emotional basket case. That evening in my little hotel room in Coral Gables, which had a single window overlooking an alley, I woke up abruptly at 3am. Through the window an incredible and intense blue light was streaming in that filled the entire room. Without question I knew this to be the presence of God, and I said aloud, "Oh, it's you God. Thank you for coming." In that moment I knew that everything would be all right. And it was. With a smile upon my face, I basked in this light until I fell asleep. The next morning I was a totally different person. We won the lawsuit handily, and a few months later, the competitor sold their business to a tire manufacturer.

A couple of years later, my wife Jill was suffering from a severe case of constipation and had scheduled exploratory surgery. In her desperation, she decided to go with her mother to visit the Unitarian Church in Pompano Beach, where a Filipino healer named Alex Orbito was scheduled to perform spiritual healings. Jill told me she was going because she was desperate and had nothing to lose. And although I wasn't sure what a spiritual healing was at this point, other than my experience in Coral Gables and my fascination with Mr. Miaggi's healing of Daniel LaRusso in the movie Karate Kid, I wished her luck, and asked her to call me when she was on the way home. I suggested we might have dinner together. So I decided to work late at the office, and at about eight thirty I called her.

"What happened honey, how'd it go?" I asked. Jill replied

very excitedly, "Oh honey, you won't believe it. That man reached right into my body, took out a lump, and I've been going to the bathroom ever since. I even had to stop three more times since I left, and I'm not even out of Pompano Beach." I replied, "Oh honey, that's great. I'm so happy for you." A moment passed and then it hit me. Puzzled, I asked, "What do you mean he reached inside of you and took out a lump?" She responded by saying, "Charles, I mean he reached right inside my stomach and took it out." Somewhat confused I asked, "Let me get this straight. He reached into your stomach, from the outside, using just his hand, and took something out of you? How is that possible?" And she said, "I don't know how he did it, but he just did it. He did similar things to at least a hundred others besides me." Now Jill was a very practical and straightforward person, and not one to spin tales. Once I questioned her at length, I never doubted what she told me. I must say that I was most intrigued with her story, and I told her that I wanted to meet this man. Jill told me that we could go to see him in Sarasota three days later, and that she would call and get the address where he would be.

Alex Orbito. Even his name sounds like something other worldly. But he's definitely human, although the healings he does can only be called divine. In the little pamphlet I read that described the beginnings of his life, it said that he had resisted this gift and had refused to use it when he was a young man. After that, his life had taken a series of bad turns and he ultimately found himself in jail. It was there that the Christ came to him and encouraged him to go out into the world and use his gift to help others, something he finally agreed to do. He was freed from jail almost immediately afterwards, and he has been doing the work ever since. In the Philippines there are a number of healers who possess this ability, the ability to reach into the body and take out damaged and diseased tissues. They call this procedure doing "openings" or magnetic healing. Other healers from Brazil like John of God and Doctor Fritz have similar abilities, something I will discuss later in this chapter.

I don't know why I was so excited at the prospect of seeing Reverend Orbito, but I was. Who wouldn't be curious about a man who could just reach into your body and take things out? Maybe it was because I felt that a man who could do such things could only receive that power from God, and maybe, just maybe, I could experience God through him. So I gathered up my little troupe to make the trip, a group consisting of Jill and I, the boys, Jill's brother Jeff, and my secretary Beth and her husband Todd. Everyone in our group with the exception of my children, Beth, and now Jill, because of her previous session, had a medical problem which the medical community could not treat successfully, and which they hoped Alex Orbito could. My own problem, although not what one would consider serious, was an un-explained pain in my upper left arm, caused I think from sleeping on it without realizing it. There was no swelling, no mark, and no evidence of any medical condition, except for the pain, which had become so severe that I could no longer sleep at night.

The home in Sarasota was located directly on the ocean, although it was a very small and humble place. At least a hundred people turned out to see Alex Orbito, some in walkers, others in wheelchairs, but mostly under their own power. It was a mild and bright sunny day, and most of us stood or sat around outside enjoying the ocean breeze while we waited our turn. Others waited inside. There was a recommended fifty dollar donation for a session, and each session took a couple of minutes at most. Alex worked on the more handicapped people first. Within a few minutes of when the healings began, I was struck by the image of an old man who walked out of the house. An hour earlier, I had seen this man struggling, using his walker and taking small, short, and sliding steps, and an interminably long time to negotiate the fifty feet of driveway that led up to the house. Now here he was walking on his own power, carrying his walker, and I swear there was a spring in his step. "What kind of magic is this," I asked myself, "where a crippled man no longer walks like a cripple?"

Eventually I made my way inside and saw the most amazing things. I watched as he literally and effortlessly opened up and invaded people's bodies, taking pieces of tissue and other anatomical parts out of them, and then watching the openings close up even more quickly than he had opened them. Even more amazing, there was no pain, little or no blood, and the people were totally comfortable and at peace. I watched him snatch cataracts out of people's eyes, broken vertebrae out of their backs, and diseased or damaged tissue out of their bodies. I saw him run his two thumbs down along the spine of one woman, like a hot knife cutting through butter, and when he reached the small of her back, I could count the vertebrae he had exposed, as her back was splayed wide open. My mouth dropped open wide as I watched the impossible. After he removed some bone fragments and pulled away his hands, her back was closed, just like that. Now you see it, now you don't. One moment her back was open, and then it wasn't. I rubbed my eyes in disbelief, as my brain was attempting to accept and compute what my eyes had just seen.

It went on like this, hour after hour, as he reached into peoples bodies and just took things out. When my own turn came, I lay upon the table they had set up and, as he started to reach for me, I grabbed his arm instead. He wasn't alarmed by this at all, and he looked into my eyes as I looked into his. I just wanted to touch him, this man of God. I just wanted to feel what that would be like. And when I did, I felt his depth and his calm and his humanity. And then I let him go. Immediately he went to the place of my pain. He penetrated into my arm with his fingers, and within moments he pulled out this yellow stringy-looking tissue which I assumed to be nerve tissue, and then showed it to me before tossing it into a collection bucket (Kimberly, who hosted and worked with Orbito for many years when he would come to Delphi, told me years later that all the body tissue he placed in the buckets would dematerialize completely within a short time afterwards). When Reverend Orbito finished, he told me in broken English to come back later in the afternoon and he would work on my liver, which I did. I can't tell you how astonishing it was to see his hands literally buried inside my stomach, and feel them moving around inside of me. When he showed me the egg-sized piece of tissue he had removed moments later, all I could think to myself was, "Do I need that?"

The pain in my arm was completely gone after that, never to return and, as far as I can tell, I didn't need that piece of liver tissue either. As I waited for the others in my group to finish their healings, I struck up a conversation with the owner of the beach house. I asked him how he had found this incredible healer and how he happened to be here. The man told me his wife was dying of cancer some years earlier. Desperate for an answer, they had found Alex, who reached into his wife and took out six large tumors, some the size of grapefruits. He said that whenever he has the opportunity, he invites Orbito to his home to work there and help others. Later that day, a young boy cut his foot on the rocks along the beach. The wound was severe and bleeding intensely. They rushed him to Rev. Orbito, who simply moved his hand once across the wound, which closed immediately. Everyone in the group casually looked at each other as if to say, "Of course, what else would we expect to happen." They had all come so far in such a short a time. This event had a dramatic and lasting impact on me too, for it restored my belief in the possibility of God, something I had struggled with since Vietnam. Interestingly, Alex Orbito used to come to Delphi every year to work until 1996, when he was no longer able to obtain a government visa. His last visit was two months before my arrival.

Although not everyone there that day was cured of their conditions, they all received some relief of their symptoms. Traditional allopathic medicine is a Godsend, particularly in surgical procedures and our ability to fight infectious disease, but in some ways it is failing and cannot succeed. What most people and our modern world don't realize is that the individual is the one who is most responsible for their own illness and their own healing. The following point is so important I will continue to repeat it. All diseases are really symptoms, symptoms of imbalance and disharmony, the result of unresolved faulty thoughts and repressed negative emotions. These thoughts and emotions affect the quality of life force energy that enters the body, create imbalances in the human energy system, and foment the conditions that allow disease to set up within the physical body. People today want to be fixed, but the truth is that only they can fix themselves. Most diseases have mental and emotional causes and require energetic and spiritual cures to truly be effective. They require understanding of the imbalance itself, and why and how it has been created. How many cancer patients go into remission, only to have the cancer reappear again months later? This is because the cause of the disease has not been cured, only the symptoms, and it simply manifests again, often in other places in the body. How many true cancer cures also reflect a change in outlook, perspective, activity, and spiritual awareness? The answer is most, if not all of them.

It was many years later, after I had come to Delphi, that I learned that there are two areas of the world most notable for psychic phenomena. The first of these was the Philippines, the home of Alex Orbito and others like him. The second and by far the most prolific is Brazil. Souls who desire to and have earned the ability to express themselves in this fashion choose to incarnate into one of these two places on earth. Simply stated, the energies there, although uniquely different from each other, are conducive to this type of expression. Both Brazil and the Philippines are remnants of the ancient spiritual continent of Lemuria, a place where spiritual capability flourished. In 1997, Kimberly and I took a trip to Brazil to visit and experience some of the healers there.

CHAPTER FOURTEEN

The Healers of Brazil

The healers of Brazil are as diverse a group as one might imagine. Two I know of have the gift of light phenomena, where actual physical lights and intense light flashes emanate directly out of their bodies. Mauricio was one of the two. The other is Thomas Green Martin, who can be found living there today. Other Brazilian healers are renowned to do major surgery using only simple utensils like scissors, scalpels, or even kitchen knives, without the benefit or need of anesthesia or operating rooms. Others like Dr. Fritz in Rio de Janeiro perform their miracles on thousands of people energetically through the use of their will and their clear intentions. Some like John of God express their healing in multiple ways. And then there was Dr. Geddes, a beer distributor by day and, when his day was done, a healer and trance channel two nights a week. When Dr. Geddes did his healings, his body was fully incorporated by the various spirit doctors with whom he worked. As is the case with so many of the healers there, he didn't charge a penny for his healings.

Dr. Geddes operated out of a small formerly converted warehouse and church building in a poor section of Sao Paolo. It was about three o'clock on a hot winter afternoon when we arrived there. A line of about a hundred people had already formed and were waiting to see him. We took our turn on line and after a time we were escorted inside. The building was sparsely appointed, with rows of church pews, a screened off seating area where a half dozen or more mediums prayed and sent energy to the patient as Dr. Geddes worked on them, and a treatment area consisting of two healing tables and a small open space. Dr. Geddes was assisted by a small number of assistants, mostly women, who asked if we could wait for our turn until everyone else was finished. They told us that the reason for this was that one of the spirit doctors, Dr. Coleman, had been an American in his last life and wanted to work on the Americans who were here today. But he had to wait until the other spirit doctors had finished their work. Of course Kimberly and I said yes, and we took a seat in the front row and watched as Dr. Geddes began his surgeries. Although Kimberly had told me what to expect, I was scarcely prepared for what I saw next.

Dr. Geddes "operated" on his patients using long, flat, and thin stainless steel needles which very much resembled barbecue skewers, only smaller, thinner, and far more delicate. These needles ranged from about six to eight inches long, less than a quarter of an inch wide, and about one sixteenth of an inch thick. The first person I saw him working on was a little girl of about seven who was accompanied by her father. The girl's left eye was swollen and distended and she clearly needed help. Before he began his work, the spirit doctor began talking and laughing with the girl's father, and they seemed very comfortable and at ease with each other. When the spirit doctor stood in front of the pair, the little girl in front and her father behind her, the unthinkable happened. I was aghast and breathless as I watched him insert the long needle directly into the girl's eye, penetrating about six inches directly into her brain. Instead of dropping dead as one should when their brain is penetrated by a steel object, this little one didn't flinch. She didn't cry, she didn't bleed, and she didn't react at all. She just smiled.

Seeing my anxiety, Kimberly pointed out the eight mediums that were also there behind a screen, channeling ectoplasm or psychic healing energy to the little girl. She went on to say that the combination of their energies and those channeled through Doctor Geddes were the reason that these things were possible. As I sat there wide-eyed and astonished, he worked on people one after one, all with the same result. I watched him cut cataracts out of eyes, do complex surgeries with little more than a knife and pair of scissors, and sew up the incisions with a needle and thread, wounds that would disappear completely within 24 hours. Few in our world would or could believe what I witnessed that day, yet these things are commonplace here and go on daily. For many it's their only source of medical care.

After seeing Dr. Geddes work on dozens of people, I finally got up the nerve to give it a try. And even though I was now "into" and being affected by the high energy there that day, I was still a little uneasy about letting him penetrate my brain and other vital body parts with the needles. So I opted instead to let him work on my knees. I had always been very athletic in my life, and these activities had taken a toll on my knees. Two previous knee surgeries failed to completely repair the damage to the meniscus cartilage under my kneecaps. As I took my turn on the table, Dr. Geddes/Dr. Coleman told a joke as he penetrated my knees with the needles. I wasn't sure if he told the joke in Portuguese or English, but I understood it just the same. As I watched him working the needles and moving them around inside of my knees, the only thing I felt was a faint pinprick, more like a tug, when they went in, and an occasional and very slight burning sensation as he worked. It was all very comfortable, simple, quick, and effective. I questioned myself for not being more trusting in the first place. The procedure was over in minutes, and there was little evidence of the surgery except for some tiny red blotches around my knees which disappeared soon after. Since that day I haven't had any further knee problems.

Perhaps the most extraordinary Brazilian healer I ever encountered was the one I never met, Mauricio Panisset, the Man of Light. Written about by Shirley McLain in her book Going Within, by Dr. Wayne Dwyer in his book Modern Magic, and by my own Kimberly in her book Man of Light, the story of her life with Mauricio, Mauricio is one of the most extraordinary individuals who has ever lived. This humble man and his spiritual legacy had a profound effect on me. In meditation and through Light Energization™ healing sessions I received from Kimberly, I was irrevocably touched by this most unique human being and his gifts of light phenomena, healing, and spiritual wisdom. Mauricio was Kimberly's late husband, and it was spiritually, through

Kimberly, that I met and came to know and love him.

Mauricio possessed the gift of light phenomena which he would use to heal others. Bright, physical lights would flash and emanate directly out of his body, out of his hands, from his heart, his third eye, and directly out of the ethers. Seeing is believing, although some who witnessed and experienced his lights firsthand, even some who were terminally ill, still didn't believe. Some even tore at his clothes in an effort to discover electrical devices or other mechanical sources of these lights. To these Mauricio would just smile humbly and ask them to leave after they were done. The lights themselves were really the manifestations of higher spiritual beings who worked through Mauricio to bring healing to others. Mauricio always responded to those in need of healing and spent his life in service to God, and the lights always responded to Mauricio and supported his healing work.

Mauricio first experienced the lights as a nine year old when they would follow him home from school. At first, he believed them to be the eyes of a panther glowing in the dark, and Mauricio would run from them. Finally, when he mustered the courage to turn and face them, he realized that these were not the eyes of an animal at all, but were physical spheres of light from a higher intelligence who communicated to him that they had come to work through him to help those in this world to heal and to awaken to a greater understanding of God and Spirit.

Mauricio resisted these lights, but it was not long afterwards, when Mauricio and his cousin were hunting, that

Mauricio unknowingly killed a pregnant animal. When he realized that the animal was pregnant, he was overcome with grief, and he prayed and called upon God to help him, promising to do anything if this animal and its' offspring could be saved. Mauricio laid his hands upon the animal in the same fashion he had seen his father do so many times before, praying and beseeching God for help. After a long time, a small blue light suddenly appeared above his hands, and then went through his hands into the body of the animal. After what felt like an eternity, the animal began to breathe and to stir. Mauricio had gotten his miracle, and he spent the rest of the afternoon rejoicing. At the evening hour, the animal suddenly got up, bolted out of the barn, and disappeared into the woods. And from that day forward, Mauricio used his gifts of light for healing.

Mauricio died in 1993 after spending but a few years together with Kimberly. Kimberly was far younger than Mauricio and the difference in their ages attracted almost as much notoriety as did the healing lights that emanated from and through Mauricio. But theirs was a great love that transcended age and time. The stories about Mauricio abound here at Delphi. Whenever Mauricio would approach his favorite restaurant and watering hole in Brasília, the Friburgo, his good friend and owner of the restaurant, Joao, would immediately pick up all the metal silverware in the restaurant and take it away, for the mere presence of Mauricio would be enough to cause the silverware to curl up and become useless. Other times Mauricio would walk along and wooden crosses would materialize out of thin air and drop on the ground behind him. He also possessed the ability of alchemy, and he could materialize medals and medallions containing biblical scenes and the pictures of saints, using only his intention. But by far the most astounding and wonderful spiritual gift he possessed was the gift of healing and light phenomena. Many say that when he performed his healing sessions, the light flashes were so intense and bright that they would cascade through windows and skylights and light up the surrounding areas and the night sky.

Kimberly has chronicled her life with Mauricio in her book, Man of Light, and in her film Manifestations of Miracles, which has actual film footage of Mauricio and other Brazilian healers expressing their gifts of light and phenomena. Today Kimberly continues this healing ministry and teaches the process of Light Energization to students of healing here at Delphi. During their time together, Kimberly served as Mauricio's apprentice, and she is the one who formalized and developed the techniques that she teaches today. Light Energization™ is far more than physical healing. It is a sacred process that raises the Kundalini up through the chakras and opens spiritual gateways which allows one to connect with one's own Higher Consciousness as well as higher levels of cosmic and divine intelligence. Through this connection, spiritual vision opens, communication with higher realms becomes possible, and a mystical experience occurs.

CHAPTER FIFTEEN

Things Are Not What They Appear to Be

Things are almost never just as they appear to be. As I reflect back upon my early life, I realize that what I had been taught or learned about God and religion didn't make much sense. Only when I began to become spiritually aware and learn the truth of spiritual and human existence did it all begin to make sense to me, perfect sense. Even as a young boy I had a very difficult time reconciling to the notion that an all-knowing, all-loving, and all-powerful God would create a world in which so many suffered. I had an even tougher time with the concept that God would give his children one chance and only one chance to "get it". And if they didn't, or if by some unlucky circumstance they just happened to die in the state of mortal sin, it was the eternal damnation of Hell's fires for them. That didn't make sense either. Who among us that love our children would or could do this? Instead, I have learned that God loves us unconditionally, despite our many faults, and we get as many chances as we need to get it right. That is the purpose and necessity of reincarnation, to discover and unfold to, and then become, our true nature and divine person. We do this through a continuing process of trial and error, of making mistakes, and making bad and then hopefully, good and better choices. Along the way, lifetime after lifetime, we start to make better choices as we begin to resonate more and more with our true divine nature. And so we keep returning to earth, along with our soul mates, friends, spiritual helpers, and family members, in different places and wearing different faces, in different guises and different costumes, in the continuous journey of spiritual evolution. We get all the chances we need to evolve to Christ Consciousness, for it takes many, many lives to discover and become the true expression of our God-nature. On the journey we get to experience this beautiful planet, its occupants, and the many gifts and attributes that God has given us.

In these next few chapters I will share much of what I have learned on my spiritual journey with you. If you are like I was, there was a time when I was so turned off by religion that I just rejected the concept on its face. Then I experienced God directly, and all bets were off. Some of the things I will share with you, you will find surprising. Others you will find profound. Ideally, everything will make sense to you, just as it has for me. Most significantly, my hope is that you will find that what I am about to share with you is both sensible and practical, for truth is simple and simply stated. For instance, there is only one ever so brief description of God in the Bible, given to us in his first book, the Gospel of John. In his most elegant and humble fashion, the disciple tells us simply that "God is love". No truth is simpler or more profound than this. I ask that, when you receive these truths, you breathe them in and take them into your heart, "feel" with them, and then decide how you feel about them. I also ask of you to keep both your mind and heart open to possibility, the possibility that we're all not just helpless and hapless victims of a cruel world, and that we all have a divine origin and purpose, one which is becoming more and more known to each of us in this, the New Day. Ask to know the truth, and you will receive it.

The Universe operates in ways that are very precise, very exact, and very mathematical. Because we live in the material world of matter and form with all of its attractions and distractions, it is very hard to discern the spiritual forces at work, or to recognize Spirit in action, particularly if you are unaware of them and aren't paying attention. Behind our helter skelter world there is a single unitary energy at work. God has a very precise plan and intention for His creation, for His children, for His own unfoldment and evolution, which He experiences collectively and through each of us, and for our own Self-awareness. All things, whether they are of the darkness or the Light, serve God's plan. Every event, every shift, every experience, and every setback are part of this unfolding plan, all according to God's will and the desire of your own Higher Self to know itself and to manifest its true divine nature on earth. Through our intention and the choices that we make, good or bad, we are either in alignment or resistance to the plan. In one way, John Calvin had it right in his Doctrine of Predestination. We are all predestined to become the expression of who we really are. Because of the quality of Divine Self Sufficiency, each of us possesses within us the ability to unfold and to know ourselves. Because we are all a part of God, each of us not only has the ability to become Self-aware, but each of us ultimately will. That's why we have come here, and why God is not preoccupied with the events of our daily lives. He knows that you will make it home because He has given you everything you need to get there, including a Higher Self, who guides you and your life's events. For some, self-awareness will happen in this lifetime. For others it will take longer, and for some it will take many more lifetimes, and perhaps, other planes of existence. But never before have the opportunities, the resources, and the energies for spiritual growth and evolution been as conducive as they are today. It's simply a question of intention, desire, and choice. You can run, but you can't hide. You can't hide from your Self indefinitely.

Prior to coming to Delphi, I developed a lump in my neck, adjacent to my throat, which was puzzling to me because I didn't know what it was. It was about the size of a pea, it wasn't very noticeable (except to me), and it didn't hurt. But nonetheless, it was there and I felt it meant something. Then one night, when I was back in Florida, I had a dream, a dream so vivid that when I awoke I felt that it had actually happened. In the dream, the first thing I saw was an open window. Shortly after I first saw it, the window slammed shut. Somehow I knew it was related, and I immediately reached for my throat to feel for the lump. I dreamt that I had returned home to Florida and my former life, and was working in advertising. Within six months the lump had developed into throat cancer and I had died. As I floated above my body I could see my wife, my children, and relatives and friends crying and mourning for me. As I lifted and joined my spiritual friends who had assembled there to greet me, I was puzzled, and I asked one of them why this had happened. He told me that I had missed my window of opportunity, and that because of this, there was no longer a reason for me to stay on earth. Immediately the realization of what he meant came flooding into me. This was not the first time I had missed the chance to fulfill my purpose. I had failed in other lifetimes as well. Determined, I set my intention not to fail this time around. Within a short time afterwards, the actual lump in my throat was completely gone.

The Universe works tirelessly to set the stage for our growth and our evolution. I have always been overwhelmed by just the thought of the energy that must go into it and the complexity and coordination necessary to accomplish all those events, activities, circumstances, conditions, chance meetings, occurrences, intricate weaves, and connections that must be met in order to insure that the life plans occur as intended. The concept itself is almost beyond human comprehension. Because of the complexities involved in setting the stage, it is not easy or even possible to recreate another opportunity in a current lifetime once the main event is missed. This is the window of opportunity. It is only open for a short time and then it closes. Typically, a new plan must be formed and another lifetime must be planned. In my own case, the Universe had painstakingly created my life, and its events had unfolded to insure that I didn't miss the opportunities we had planned at a soul level. As if to validate my actions, the dream was showing me what would happen if I turned back. I had come into this lifetime to express my spirit. The energy center of expression is in the throat. Because I had failed to express my true nature and my purpose for being here, I created an imbalance in my throat chakra and in my being which then manifested itself as cancer, and a quick exit. I knew that I could only go forward, and I couldn't go back.

And so, my apprenticeship at Delphi complete, I have now embarked upon this book to share with you what I've learned. I have learned so many wonderful and astonishing things. Life now makes sense to me, and I understand so much. And yet I still know so little. When you receive my words, be open to possibility. Be open to receive God's love and wisdom, for which I am merely one of His many humble servants. And finally, be open to a new way of perceiving yourself as far more than just a human being, at the mercy of the world, and powerless to heal or help yourself. For the truth is you are more, much more. Continue reading and see. Oh, and one more thing. As I said at the outset of this book, when you receive these teachings, take them into your heart. Put your mind aside for a few moments and trust your feelings. Just breathe into your heart and feel if what I have to say feels right. Ask to know the truth, and you will receive it. Just trust your feelings, and you will know the truth of who you are, the truth of you.

CHAPTER SIXTEEN

Who am I, What am I, and What the heck am I doing here?

This is the big question, isn't it? Who, what, and where am I? It's the one man has pondered since the beginning of his human existence, "Who am I?" Most of us think of ourselves as just a body, at the mercy of and often the victim of a merciless world. Soul is something people hope exists, and Spirit is an abstract concept. But you're far more than just a physical being. Much, much more.

You are a true child of God. You are not a creation, not something outside the essence we call God, but a piece of God's Light itself. If God is an ocean, and you were to dip a cup into that ocean, what resides in the cup is you, your consciousness or Higher Self, no different than the water from which it was drawn, except a part of you is actually contained in a cup or container. Think of this cup as your body and personality. Think of the rest of you as Spirit, made in the image and likeness of God. More about that later.

You are a Spiritual Being trying to be Human, not the other way around. You already have that spiritual part figured out. It's what you are. Your very essence is spirit. It's the human part, first developing a sense of self, and then evolving the unevolved or little self into the big or Higher Self that we're all trying to work out. You have an Eternal Consciousness, without beginning or end. Everything that ever was, is, or ever will be, has always been contained within the heart of God, including you and me. What does an eternal being do with eternity and an unlimited source of energy, and a God who by His very nature multiplies and expands Himself in an incalculable number of expressions and forms?

In order to know who we are, we must also know God, because the search for Self is the search for God, the search for God is the search for Self. When Yahweh (God the Father, pronounced "Yah-Vey") chose to experience all aspects of *Himself*, and express *Herself* in matter, the human idea had begun (please notice my accent on the twin aspects of God here, which are both male and female). Remember that everything that ever was, is, or will be, including each of us has always been contained within the Heart and Mind of God. The ultimate purpose on earth of each and every one of us is to bring our Spirit, our Higher Selves, God's Spirit, fully into matter. Made in the Image of God means that we are Spirit. Made in the likeness of God means we have the same exact abilities, primary of which is our ability to create and manifest our thoughts into form and reality.

"And God said; Let us make man in our image,
after our likeness" Genesis 1:26

Notice the use of the words "*us*" and "*our*" from this passage in the Book of Genesis. It is clear that God had already begun His expression in the form of Holy Monads or Elohim, known as the Creator Gods, who were the first direct expressions and projections out of the Godhead, our first ancestors, and whose role it was to begin the building of the worlds and its future life forms. Once matter is formed, then Spirit can occupy it. This is also true of our own physical bodies. Each of us begins our existence as a Holy Monad. The Monads are then impulsed by the Creator, allowing them the choice of expressing themselves into the Worlds of Form. And just like their Creator, the Monads project parts of themselves into time and space, reducing and stepping down their energies so that they may condense into more physical energy forms.

The Monad ultimately projects a number of Permanent Personalities through which they themselves and God experience life and the attractions of the physical world. The total of the projections from each Monad are known as its Soul Group, which is composed of all the individual expressions of the Monad as the personalities which typically travel together and provide the earthly experiences for each other that they desire and need, according to their individual life plans, consistent with the Divine Plan. The members of the Soul Group are also known as Soul Mates, and the groups themselves can be extremely large. Members of each group tend to reincarnate together, and they often change roles from lifetime to lifetime. A daughter may have been her mother's mother in another lifetime, or a father could be a brother, sister, child, husband or wife in another. The possibilities are endless, especially considering that a large number of us, the Old Souls, have lived thousands of lifetimes on the earth. When an individual desires or needs an experience which his own soul group cannot provide, he incarnates into another group for that lifetime which can provide what he needs.

The Permanent Personality is known as the Higher Self. The Higher Self is the *Image* of God, the Spirit and essence of who you really are. The Higher Self creates the Soul, which it uses to experience life and the physical world. Each of us is the projection of our Higher Self. This projection is known as the Temporary Personality. The Temporary Personality is manifested through the interaction of the Higher Self and the feminine aspect of God, the Holy Spirit. Each Temporary Personality comes into life with a plan. This plan typically includes earthly experiences, spiritual growth and evolution, and the discharge and balancing of one's karma. The Temporary Personality lives only one lifetime. At death, the Temporary Personality merges back with its Soul or what is also known as the Soul Body. The Soul itself is the collection of all the memories and experiences of all the Temporary Personalities which have been projected by the Higher Self through all of its earthly incarnations. The reason you can experience past lives is because of these soul memories.

Think of your Soul as a new car or vehicle maker. Each lifetime you fashion and receive a new car, a physical body, in which to experience the upcoming incarnation. This new car is furnished with all the options, characteristics, and even the shortcomings you will need to fulfill your life's plan. At the end of your life, the car is worn out and ideally, the plan is fulfilled, which is solely dependent on what you do or don't do in that lifetime, based upon the choices you make or don't make. Free will and free choice is given to the Temporary Personality to follow or not to follow the stirrings of the Higher Self. Spiritual and soul evolution is therefore dependent upon the thoughts, feelings, and actions of the Temporary Personality. At death you return to the Astral World where you are reunited with your soul and all of the memories of all of your previous Temporary Personalities. After attending schools of higher learning, you plan your upcoming life with a lot of help from your spiritual friends, and you receive a new vehicle to drive.

It is the desire of the Higher Self to merge with and fully embody its physical projection or Temporary Personality, it's soul, which is you and I. In order for this to happen, we must prepare the Temple of the Body by healing and transmuting negative thought patterns, feelings, and limiting behaviors, most of which have been created in previous lifetimes, so that the Temple is fit to receive the full embodiment of God through the incorporation of the Higher Self. This event is popularly known as Ascension, the ascension of the Temporary personality with the Permanent Personality or Higher Self. But in reality it is the Descension of the Higher Self and merger with its projection or Temporary Personality.

God's Plan is to form and then express Himself in Matter; to scatter an incalculable number of his individual expressions into the physical worlds as personalities, to experience these personalities through their expressions and their own experiences, and then for these personalities to evolve and find their way back to God or Christ Consciousness through their own free will, free choice, and God desire. In order for the plan to work, it was necessary for man to separate himself from his Source. And although each of us has experienced this separation in one form or another, we have always maintained an energy connection with God and our Higher Selves through our Etheric or Life Body, which enables or enabled us to reconnect with Spirit when the time was right. Moreover, in order to develop a sense of self or ego, each of us had to begin by being selfish. Selfishness was a necessary part of the Divine Plan. However, once the ego is formed, it must then be evolved. So the path of human evolution is to evolve from selfishness to selflessness, from taking to giving, from conditional to unconditional love. As evolving god-men and god-women, we must change our desires and our Desire Body from selfish interests to the Desire Body of God, which only wants good for all things. It takes many, many lifetimes to become Self-aware, to discover, grow, and evolve into your GodSelf which is the state of Christ Consciousness, a fully awake, fully aware, Christ Conscious human being. This is the ultimate expression, purpose, and destiny of each and every one of us, and is the reason why incarnation is necessary

Many have wondered, including me, why God chose to come out, to come out of the void and into expression. And if you recall, everything that ever was, is, or will be has always been contained within the Mind of God, including you and me. So one day I asked Him directly, point blank, and I said: "Okay God, give it up. Tell me true. Why did you come out?" And immediately He gave me the answer, and He said it so eloquently and yet so simply: "Charles, I just couldn't contain my Self ". Wow. How beautiful is truth? So simple, so elegant, and so simply stated.

CHAPTER SEVENTEEN

Principles of Energy

If you are going to truly understand how things work, you will need a basic understanding of the Principles of Energy. I'm not talking about oil, or natural gas, electricity, wind, or solar power. I'm talking about the fundamental and first rule of being, which is:

> "Everything is energy"
> Albert Einstein

Everything that exists is energy in one form or another. And if it's energy, it's in a state of vibration and is putting out a sound. The fundamental differences between one form of energy and another can be characterized by four basic things:

1. Density – how tightly or loosely the cells, molecules, atoms, and subatomic particles are packed together

2. Frequency – the rate of vibration

3. Sound – the sound created by the vibratory rate.

4. Characteristics – visible, invisible, tangible, intangible, strength, feel, mental, emotional, physical, spiritual

If something exists, it is vibrating and putting out a sound, even though we can't usually hear it. The sound or rate of vibration is known as its frequency. Very high energies resonate very high frequencies. With very low energies the opposite is true. All matter is the result of higher energies or frequencies, the thoughts of the divine, which have been lowered or stepped down in order to condense and come into form. It is sound vibration that caused matter to form up into regular patterns, and sound or "the word" is the basic energy driver of manifestation. When the masculine energy of sound is expressed, it is the creator of light, its opposite, the feminine energy.

Energy is also the things we don't see

Energy is also the things we don't see, but often can feel and experience, particularly if you're in touch with your spiritual gifts. Energies like love, emotions, thoughts, feelings, anger, fears, intentions, wisdom, and anything else that are not tangible still exist in a different vibratory or energy state. An aware person can often sense and see these energies which evade the five senses. You can't see air, yet it sustains you and keeps you alive. You can't see electricity either, but if you put your finger in a live electrical socket, you will then "see" the truth.

Energy is created and responds instantly to thought and

feeling. Moreover one can direct energy to act as you think or want it to be. Therefore the next rule of energy is this:

"As you think it, so it will be"
Mauricio Panisset

You can direct energy to act as you want or expect it to do. As Mauricio Panisset used to say, "As you think it, so it will be". A group of scientists can all perform the same experiment, under the same exact conditions, and yet each can come up with a different result. Why? Because each one had a different intention and expectation, and the results obtained were consistent with what they believed and wanted to happen. Subsequently, each one created what they wanted and expected through their creative intention, although each result was different. This is why scientific experiments are validated both for reliability and validity. Just because a result holds true for one does not insure that this is true for others. The same holds true with drug experiments and placebos. Some of those taking the faux-medicine placebos also were healed, solely because they thought they would be.

This application of energy, the power of thought and intention, can be very easily distinguished in the process of healing. Today's modern energy healer can think and direct energy into a client's body through their thoughts and intentions, their breath, through their hands, and from higher realms. But they can also direct healing energy to travel to someone halfway around the world and be very effective, just as if they were there physically. The only limitation to the use and direction of energy is preconceived thinking and personal capability and experience.

When my mom was still with us, I would end each phone conversation we had by sending her love over the phone. She told me afterwards that the phone would get so hot that she couldn't hold onto it. On another occasion, I was on vacation in Italy and called my children to check in and say hello. As I prepared to say goodbye to my son Michael, I told him that I was going to send him my love. Immediately he felt it, and within moments he said, "Dad, what are you doing? Please stop it. You're scaring me". The next principle of energy is the Law of Attraction:

Like attracts like

Unlike electricity where opposites attract; in the universe, in the use of energy, like attracts like. Love is attracted to love. Fear is attracted to fear. Each of us is a big energy broadcaster. We are constantly putting thoughts, feelings, and vibrations out into the world that are resonating one form of energy or another. Our world is densely packed with thoughtforms and spiritual beings of both higher and lower energies. These energies are attracted to things that are like themselves or to things that they desire. On a more practical level, each of us will draw to ourselves the energies, people, places, events, and circumstances that we are attracting, according to what we're resonating or putting out.

To access different forms of energy, one need only ask for them to come. This is called:

The Power of Invocation

One method I use is to invoke the energies of healing is by using the many names of God in Hebrew. Hebrew is a divine language, not of this earth, which was imparted to Abraham by Archangel Michael. In Hebrew, God is called by His attributes, of which He has many. The names of God in Hebrew are really a series of thoughtforms which when resonated create the vibration of the name. So if I resonate the phrase "God is your healer" in Hebrew, I am invoking the healing energy of God. The vibration of the name creates the delivery of the attribute of the name. Essentially, what I'm doing is resonating the vibration and then attracting that vibration to me.

At Delphi, we begin each healing session with a simple invocation:

"I ask to be used as a channel of love, light, and healing"

This is a simple yet most powerful method of invoking the healing energies. Offer yourself to God to use, and the Universe will send the energies of love, light, and healing to you so that you can channel and share them with others.

Unlike ordinary people, the spiritually aware person knows that they're more than just a body, much more. The truth of being the human being is this:

You are an energy system

Composed of your physical, etheric, emotional, and mental bodies, your chakras, kundalini, energy meridians, and auric field, and your three spiritual bodies, you are an energy system. All facets of you are designed to work in harmony with each other. An unhealthy energy system is like a symphony orchestra with one or more pieces playing out of tune.

The final energy principle I will speak of is:

God is an unlimited source of energy.

There is no limit to the energies of God. The greatest energy reserves in the Universe lie within the Heart and Mind of God. God is an inexhaustible storehouse of energy. To create it, all He has to do is think it. You are much the same. You also create with your thoughts and your intentions, and you can access the various energies of God simply by asking for and then using them. Not matter what you need, you can access it. No matter what you want, if you can image it you can create it. Your own thoughts have the power to bring the energy into form or function. God gives us access to all of His energies of love, creation, transmutation, and manifestation, provided we know how to obtain and use them wisely. God's energy is endless.

CHAPTER EIGHTEEN

Life's Journey, Purpose, Plan, & Our Spiritual Anatomy

The Human Idea began when God decided to express Himself in matter. Coming out of the void or from a non-manifest state, God reflected upon Himself and beheld his reflection, his opposite, his feminine nature and counterpart. From that reflection Christ Consciousness, the personality of God, was birthed and expressed, and the Plan of Creation went forward. There are three aspects to the Godhead or Holy Trinity. The first of these is the Father who wills things into existence. The second is the Christ aspect, the personality of God, who provides the wisdom, personalities, and the plan of creation. The third aspect of the Trinity is known as the Holy Spirit or Divine Mother which is the feminine expression of God that manifests divine thought into form. God is androgynous, both male and female, as are each of us. One has only to look around in the world to see it, to recognize the divine role fulfilled by the Holy Spirit, the feminine aspect of the Trinity, the manifestor of life, and the constructor of the worlds. And even though we can identify these three different aspects of the Godhead, they are still just One and always work together in wisdom, love, and power. God wills it, the Christ energy plans it, and the Holy Spirit executes the plan in combination with the Christ energy, according to the will of the Father.

The first step in God or Human expression was the projection of parts of Himself as Holy Monads to begin, direct, and fulfill the divine plan. The second step in Creation was the formation of the worlds. Once matter is manifested, Spirit in its many forms begins to occupy it and then to evolve it. Only in expression does one have individual existence. Only in matter, only by being able to distinguish oneself from one's environment and surroundings can one develop an ego and an individual identity, a sense of self. Before we came into expression, the only being who possessed an ego was God. In expression there are now many selves or egos operating within and according to the Human Idea. We are many, yet we are one. As it was at the beginning and is now, the only true reality is the Light of God shining behind and through all things. Everything else is an illusion. Because we believe we are separate from God, the practical reality is that we are, at least in our own minds. Our thoughts and feelings create our reality.

The Human Journey continued with the formation of the stars and cosmic systems, and ultimately our own Solar System. Our Earth Mother, a great spiritual being known as Gaia, provides the sustenance for our existence, and has had three previous incarnations, the present one as the Earth being the fourth and the latest. All of our ancestors, from the Great Monads and Archangelic presences to the ultimate unfolding and end result in the Divine Plan, the human being, have taken part and participated in the Human Idea, the plan of existence, of God experiencing himself.

The Earth is not the first place we came and upon which we incarnated. It is simply the latest and the most recent. As our Solar System formed and developed, there were a number of earlier formations that preceded the final formation that we know today. These formations or cycles were necessary prerequisites to the ultimate formation of the Earth and those who would occupy it, and we and our ancestors, from the highest to the lowest, actively participated in this development. Although God's plan was perfect, the plan had to be executed, and the human forms we occupy today had to be created from scratch, and had to follow a long evolutionary trail to completion. These energy forms not only include the physical body, but also the three subtle bodies: etheric, mental, and emotional, the faculties which man would need for his ultimate expression as an ego bearer on Earth.

In the fires of Ancient Saturn man developed an Etheric or Life Body, which was and continues to be animated to this day by the energy of the Holy Spirit, the feminine aspect of the Godhead. The Etheric Body is sometimes referred to as the Vital Body, and is an exact energetic double of the physical body. The Etheric Body contains a template of each and every atom, cell, molecule, organ, and body part. It is the Etheric Body that animates the physical body and gives it life, and it is the Etheric Body that withdraws at death. The living tissue of man, and all living things, exists only because of the Etheric Body supporting it. Science cannot create life because it has no way to create a spiritually-based energy body, the Etheric Body. All dis-ease and imbalance manifests first in the etheric body before it enters the physical. Additionally, because the Etheric Body is the blueprint of the physical body, they are very closely related. Any trauma to the physical body will also affect the Etheric Body (i.e. physical injuries, holes in the aura). The Etheric Body is also the vessel through which our connection with God and Spirit has been maintained through the ages. No matter how far away from Spirit that man has travelled or distanced himself, he has always maintained his connection with the Light, and access to the Grace of God. This connection was also essential for man to reawaken to his Spirit when the time and circumstances were right.

On the Ancient Sun, man developed his Mental or Causal (thoughts cause action) Body which gave him the ability to think, to reason, to make choices, and most importantly, enabled him to form his own individual identity, ego, and sense of self. In the watery environment of the Ancient Moon, man developed his Emotional/Astral or Desire Body. This body enables man to feel and experience feelings and desires. It contains the patterns, feelings, and vibrations that determine our personality, how we feel about ourselves, and how we interact with others. Because man is equipped with both Mental and Emotional bodies, he is able to choose the thoughts and feelings he wants, all consistent with his free will.

As the rudiments of all of the life forms that would ultimately manifest on Earth were being formed through sound vibration in the waters of the Ancient Moon, man lived in a dream consciousness and acted out being human in his dreams, even though he didn't yet have a physical body. Just like today, when a dream can be so strong that when we awaken we think it actually happened, man's dreams on the Ancient Moon became his reality and man became increasing dependent upon them. In these dreams he was able to act out being human, and able to express and establish his lower desires repeatedly, which ingrained them into his consciousness. When man ultimately received his human form, he hit the ground running.

Finally, after his descent onto the Earth, man developed his dense material form or Physical Body, the one we know today, but only after many thousands of years of earth life and selfish expression. It is in the physical body that we experience life, and it is the physical body that is the recipient of all influences from the subtle bodies, good or bad. The physical body has never had a faulty thought or unbalanced emotion, the precursors to disease. But since it's the receiver of all subtle influences, the physical body "takes the hit" or the negative effect for the team, and reflects this imbalance in appearance or effect. Most of mankind thinks of themselves as only a physical body. But the human being is composed of many bodies, each having a different yet related role and effect. When man dies, he leaves here what he received here, the hard mineral and material form. "Ashes to ashes, and dust to dust".

The human anatomy is really an energy system, composed of your subtle or energy bodies, your physical body, your chakras, and the energy meridians of the physical body.

The Subtle Bodies extend around the physical body. The closest of these is the Etheric or Life Body which penetrates throughout and extends about one inch outside the physical body. The Emotional Body extends out about one to three inches, and the Mental Body approximately three to eight inches from the physical. These energy emanations change very frequently and can extend much further depending upon the mental and emotional activity of the individual, his physical condition, his mood, his evolutionary state, and his environment. The combination of all the energies emanating from the bodies is called the Aura or Auric Field, which changes from moment to moment.

Your subtle bodies serve to coordinate and regulate the soul's activities in life. When there is a misalignment of the subtle bodies with the physical body, psychological and physical problems result. Therefore for true healing to occur, we must treat the physical, mental, emotional, as well as the spiritual bodies of the individual. An imbalance in any of the subtle bodies will ultimately manifest in the physical body. The physical body is the receiver of all subtle influences, and the creator of none of them. Protracted and reinforced faulty thoughts and unbalanced emotions are the true cause of imbalance and dis-ease.

Additionally, as a human being you also have three spiritual bodies, the Holy Monad, Eternal Self-Aware Soul (not to be confused with the human soul), and the Higher Self. The closest of the spiritual bodies is known as the Higher Self. The Higher Self possesses Christ Consciousness and is God. It is your own personal piece of God, the one to whom you pray and the same one that directs your life.

Using my earlier example, if God were an ocean and you were to dip a cup into this ocean, what remains in the cup is your Higher Self, possessing the same abilities, the same aspects, and the same consciousness as the Creator. The Higher Self and God are one, just as you and your Higher Self are one. The Higher Self projects a Temporary Personality, YOU, through which to experience earth life, and to express Spirit in matter. This temporary personality, this human being, has complete Free Will, and is able make its own choices, and suffers the effects of these choices, good or bad.

Your ultimate expression is the merger of you and your Higher Self as one. This is also known as Ascension, but is really the Descension and merger of the Higher Self with the physical form. This condition is also known as Self-Enlightenment, Self Realization, or Christ Consciousness. When your role in the plan is finished you will once again be one with your Higher Self. You will not lose yourself but rather, you will gain the rest of you. Your consciousness will not only continue but now in its highest expression.

When God unfolded Himself out of the Godhead he first projected parts of Himself as the Holy Monads. Each of us begins as a Holy Monad. These Monads projected parts of themselves into matter, in the form of the Self-Aware Souls; some forming the celestial and planetary bodies, and others forming the life forms that would ultimately oc-cupy the matter that they formed. From the Self-Aware Souls, God projected and expanded Himself further into the Permanent Personalities or Higher Selves.

The four cycles of planetary formation and man's development on Ancient Saturn, the Ancient Sun, the Ancient Moon, and the Ancient Earth took millions of years to accomplish and not only were established for the development of his form, but also his Subtle Bodies, and ultimately his ego and sense of self. For any spiritual being to have and develop a sense of self, they must come into expression. On Ancient Saturn we began the development of the life body and our future form. On the Ancient Sun we initiated the development of the mind and our ability to think. On the Ancient Moon we developed emotions and desires, and the etheric template of our physical forms. And now we find ourselves on the Earth, spiritual beings trying to be physical, not the other way around.

So, what's the purpose of our existence? There are many. First, we come into physical form so that we can create something that hitherto only God possessed, and that is an individualized ego and sense of self. In Oneness, before expression, only God possesses a sense of self. Our challenge on the pathways of life is to perfect that individual ego and awareness into a state of Christ Consciousness. Second, we come here to experience life, to experience the physical world, something which we cannot do as pure Spirit. Whatever we experience becomes a permanent part of our consciousness. Third, an important part of each of our life plans, the plan we make each time we come into a new incarnation, is to discharge our karma, to balance and heal the imbalances we have created over lifetimes, and to forgive ourselves and obtain forgiveness from others, whether directly or indirectly. Fourth, we come to heal and express ourselves and our Spirit/Higher Self in the physical world, and to prepare the body temple to merge with the Higher Self, the ultimate human condition, the state of Christ Consciousness. Fifth, fully embodied by the Higher Self, we express our highest gifts of love, light, and healing. And sixth, in so doing, we come to expand God's presence in the physical world through our own presence and the expression of our love.

All beings, great and small, play an integral role in the Plan of Creation. Everything that happens in life has meaning and spiritual purpose. For you see, the Universe is not divided by rank, but by function, with each of us, no matter how great or how small, playing our unique and essential role. The greatest archangel and the simplest human being are no different in the Eyes of God. God loves us perfectly, each and every one.

One day I was speaking to God and telling Him about my problems. And then it occurred to me that I was rambling on and wasting His time. And so I said, "Forgive me Father. I know you have better things to do than to listen to my story." And then He answered me, an answer I hardly expected, and one which I heard as clear as day. "I have heard many stories Charles, but I have loved no other better than yours." And in that instant I knew, I knew and I realized how much God loves each and every one of us, for he didn't say I had the best story. But rather, He told me that my story was important, just as important as any other. And I knew then, that not only was my story important, but that I was important to Him too. And so are you.

CHAPTER NINETEEN

Eternal Life, the Myths of Death, and of Heaven and Hell

Although God is one, there are three aspects to the Godhead, each of which provide a necessary function, all of which also act in concert. God the Father is masculine aspect and He expresses this energy fundamentally as Divine Will. God "wills" all things into existence. The second aspect of the Godhead or Trinity is what we call Christ Consciousness or the Personality of God. The Christ aspect is the planner and the personality of creation. The third aspect of God and the most prolific is the Feminine aspect, also known as the Holy Spirit, Divine Mother, or the Shekinah. The Divine Mother manifests all things into existence, consistent with the plan of the Christ Energies according to the will of the Father.

As God unfolds Himself out of the Godhead, He projects parts of Himself out into the Universe, into the worlds of form, according to the Divine Plan. Fundamentally, the Divine Plan is God projecting Himself into matter and then finding his way back home, through his own free will and free choice, navigating through the forces of attraction, resistance, and limitation, back to his heart, his true divine nature, and ultimately the rediscovery and embodiment of who he really is. The ultimate projection of Divine Light is man. The ultimate and final expression of man is the state of Christ Consciousness. Your Higher Self directs your life and your plan, and it uses the soul as the vessel or vehicle in which to experience the physical world and express itself in matter. We are the bridge that connects Spirit and Matter. The soul itself is the combination of all the Temporary Personalities expressed by the Higher Self throughout time, and the Higher Self will continue to send its personalities, its soul, into the world of time and space until it attains Christ Consciousness, the state in which God is fully present and expressed in matter. Once the journey is complete, the Soul and the Higher Self will merge as one.

And so the Higher Self projects a part of itself into form, into matter, in the form of Temporary Personalities, just as God projects the Higher Self. You live many lifetimes, assuming many different roles, and experiencing many different things. God experiences himself through each of us. God knows exactly how you think and feel, because He is you. The journey isn't over until you complete it, and you get as many chances as you need to attain Christ Consciousness. This is why reincarnation occurs and why it is essential. The journey is extensive and at times very difficult. But what you gain from it and through it is an evolved Ego and an individualized personality, someone who is both God or Christ Conscious, and also an individual Ego bearer. You will never lose this self nor your experience, for this is really who you are. When the journey is complete you gain the rest of yourSelf which is God, and God multiplies and enriches Himself through each of us. In the Italian language you'll find the names Dino and Dina which mean Little God and Little Goddess. This is our true potential.

Made in the Image and Likeness of God means you are the same. The Image of God is Spirit, and each of us are truly spirit. Our bodies and temporary personalities will last only as long as they're needed for each lifetime, but our Permanent Personality or Higher Self is eternal. Made in the likeness of God means we have the same abilities as God, the foundation of which is Divine Self Sufficiency, the power of creation. Just like your Creator, you have within you everything that you need to become and express your own divine person, to create the life you desire. The powers given to you by God the Father are the same as he uses Himself: Will, Intention, and Love. This power, the ability to will your thoughts into reality, is the ultimate power in the Universe. *You are the creator of your life and ultimately your world*. Change your mind, change your thoughts, and you will change your life.

We came to the earth and manifest here in our Soul Groups. Remember the Monad from which we were first projected? The total of the projections of each Monad result in the expression of our individual soul groups. We travel and incarnate primarily with other members of our soul groups who provide all the experiences, circumstances, acts, and events we need to grow, and to experience and express human life. It is common to change roles regularly in these expressions. I can be a man in one life, a woman in another.

I could be my father's son or my mother's daughter in the next, or I can be their parent, their good friend, or even their tormentor. We typically get the experience we need from within our own soul groups. When what we need for a subsequent life cannot be provided by our own group, we temporarily incarnate into a different group that can give us what we need.

After each incarnation we return to one of the levels of the Astral Plane, which is divided according to our levels or grades of consciousness or evolutionary status. The higher one's individual awareness, the higher the level one ascends to after death. As John Lennon stated so eloquently, imagine there's no heaven and no hell. There are only way stations in the journey of perfect being and perfect becoming. In the Astral World there are seven levels, which have also been called the Seven Heavens. The upper levels of the Astral Plane are what we would call Heavenly, although the bliss, joy, and experiences found there are far beyond even our slightest comprehension of what heaven would be like. The middle levels are a lot more like the earth and, except for level four which many would liken to the human concept of heaven, are fundamentally astral duplications of earth and earth-like environments. It is on these levels, levels two and three, where most of the world's people go when they die.

The lowest level of the Astral, known as Avichi, is the place of unrestrained power and selfish desire. It is the equivalent of what we know as hell, but unlike our traditional understanding of Hell, it's not a place of eternal damnation and punishment, but rather it's a more purgatorial environment. Avichi is the place of unfulfilled desires. Unlike the other areas of the Astral in which one can feel and experience things and fulfill their higher desires, the occupants of Avichi have no way to fulfill their lower desires and passions. It is a place reserved exclusively for only the most incorrigible and wicked of humanity, a place which no ordinary person will ever touch or experience. In Avichi, the desires ultimately die for lack of fulfillment, and the occupant, if and when ready, will once again get a chance to reincarnate and travel the spiritual path.

God does not punish you. You are quite good at that yourself, particularly from a subconscious level. God doesn't get angry or upset, nor is He disappointed or sad with you either. God doesn't express lower human emotions. He is the essence of love and goodness. In your journey you will be given as many chances as you need to figure it all out, and to discover and become who and what you really are. God isn't worried that we may not find our way back Home either, for we possess the same powers and abilities that He does. God impels us quietly and subtlety. He gives us free will and free choice to follow or not to follow the path. He knows who you are and what you are, and He knows that one day you'll return to Him, only far more evolved and experienced than when you first left the comfort of your celestial surroundings, the Prodigal Son returned home. As an eternal being, without beginning or end, what would you do with eternity? Many of us have chosen to enter the Human Idea, to follow God's plan of Self-realization, experiencing life in all its many facets, living in and marveling at the wonders of the earth, and developing our conscious awareness, evolving from the little self to the Big Self. And here we are.

CHAPTER TWENTY

The Forces of Resistance or Evil

There is only One God, only one driving force that operates in the Universe, and that is God's Will, and His power and His will are absolute. Everything that exists is within Absolute Being, and this state of being or Absolute Beingness is God. Nothing exists or operates outside of the Godhead, or stands against His will. God has everything he needs to be God, and you have within you, everything you need to be you. God has endowed each of us with his own abilities such as Divine Self Sufficiency. Through this energy you can create or attain whatever you need, such that you have everything you need to discover and unfold to your own divine person. But this energy is so powerful that, left to its own devices, it would soon become self-aware, and the Plan of Creation would come to a premature conclusion. Because of this, the Forces of Resistance were also included as part of the Divine Plan as a counterbalance to the full potential of Divine Self Sufficiency. It is from these forces of darkness, of resistance, of evil, of trial and error that we learn. By making mistakes, by rejecting what doesn't work or those things which we're not, we discover who we really are. During the unfolding of the Divine Plan, a group of Archangelic Forces, operating under the direction of the Christ Energies, were adversely commanded, who sacrificed themselves and provided obstacles to the course of human spiritual evolution, so that God's plan could be fulfilled.

There are a number of resistive forces operating in the world, and although they seem to be and are evil on their face, they perform their roles according to the Plan of the Christ and the Will of the Father. The first group of these is the archetypal energies, which were first loosed by the beings of light, and then freed once again when the Christ descended into the Astral Hells. These energies are the energies of power, distraction, and temptation. We first experienced these energies in our Moon evolution when we lived in a dream or picture consciousness. Our consciousness was literally overwhelmed by these archetypes, and there was no way to resist their continuous influence. In this dream consciousness, we perfected the shortcomings of human behavior long before we had physical bodies. These archetypes are still very active today and affect all people until they learn to overcome them.

The second group of resistive forces is the Forces of Limitation under the Luciferic Powers. The Forces of Limitation don't want you to discover or express your own light or your own divine person. Their mission is to prevent you from doing that. They want to limit and control you by making your choices for you, and they exercise this power through group control. They want everyone in the group to be the same, to act the same, and to receive the same in the manner they direct. The Forces of Resistance don't want you to evolve spiritually and discover who you really are. Rather they want to hold you down, unevolved spiritually, and just keep us all the same, unaware and un-empowered. You will never hear from them until you begin to shine your light, and their role is to make sure that you don't. One only has to look around at the current world to see this energy at work in socialist governments, redis-tributive economic policies, dogmatic religious institutions, and political philosophy.

The Satanic Forces, on the other hand, want to take away your comforts, your possessions, and what you love. They want to take everything away from you to demonstrate that you know and believe nothing, that there is no God. In the Book of Job, God assembles a council of his advisors, one of whom is Satan. God sees that Satan is troubled, and so he asks what's wrong. Satan answers that God gave him a job to do, but he can't do his job because God won't let him touch His children. God recognizes this and allows Satan to directly affect Job in stages, although he is ordered not to kill him. And although Satan first takes Job's possessions, then his loved ones, and finally his health, Job remains loyal and devoted to God, though he doesn't understand why bad things happen to good people and vice versa. But he believes there is divine purpose in everything, even in misfortune, which is one of the primary ways people re-discover God. In the end, Job is rewarded "doubly" for his steadfast faith and devotion.

The last of the resistive forces I'll mention are the Ahrimanic Forces, which one could call evil in their nature and in their effect. These forces provide the impetus for selfish desires and fear-based expressions. The focus of the Ahrimanic energies is materialism and the material world, and the energies of greed, lust, power, and desire. They operate through deception, by denying or ignoring the true spiritual nature of the human being, and they thrive on sowing conflicts between different groups of people and getting them to attack one another. They promote fear and fear-mongering and they attempt to control group thoughts, attitudes, and behaviors. The Forces of Ahriman will place great emphasis on education, on mathematics and science for instance, but will use them as false truths and barriers to truth, believing only in science at the expense of reason.

The idea of evil itself is really a misconception. People are inherently good, not evil, although they often act that way. What many people don't realize or accept is that God really does exist, and God is truly God. All of creation operates under his watch, both the good and what we often refer to as evil. God is the Source of all things. There is no power that rivals or stands against the Godhead. The darkness, the Forces of Resistance are energies designed to help us discover our true selves and our true light, by forcing us to move through our earthly limitations, and to overcome the distractions of the material world and our lower nature through the exercise of our free choice and free will. Through many lifetimes each of us has played the role of the persecuted and the persecutor. Only when we face and uncover our shadows do we discover the truth of who we really are. The Forces of Resistance serve God's will and God's Plan by teaching us to realize and choose what we want and what we don't want. By working through and navigating the obstacles, and by making mistakes and ultimately more enlightened choices, we are finally able to discover our own divine nature and the God within ourselves.

CHAPTER TWENTY-ONE

The Law of Karma, of Divine Balance, of Cause and Effect

There is a law that operates in the Universe, the Law of Karma, or the Law of Cause and Effect, that really governs human behavior. The Ten Commandments weren't rules of behavior. They were Karmic Laws which stated simply that if you violate a commandment you would also suffer the same effects yourself. The Old Testament admonition, "An eye for an eye, and a tooth for a tooth" was also a statement of karmic effect, and not an authorization for revenge. The Law of Karma, also known as the Law of Divine Balance, is about cause, effect, and about being responsible for what you do. If you cause something to happen, the effect is that you are responsible for it. Typically this is about causing harm to another, although this may also apply to other things. Under the Laws of Karma, the Law of Divine Balance, you are responsible for what you do, and it's up to you to make it right. Typically, a murderer is ultimately murdered, whether in this life or another. One of the most serious karmic events is to deny the opportunity for a person to live and express life, and to deny them their choices and their opportunities for spiritual growth. When you deny someone their life choices, you take on their karma. This can also happen when a parent tries to shelter their child and deny them their life's experiences.

Some believe that a karmic violation causes a tear in the Astral Plane which can only be repaired by the one who caused it. Anything you do that causes harm to another or denies them freedom of choice is a karmic event, and you will carry this karma with you, lifetime after lifetime, until you heal or balance it out. A large part of the life plans we bring in with each incarnation is directed towards balancing our karma, and to heal those things we have created. Karma can be created and healed in a number of ways.

We create karma with our actions, our words, our thoughts, and our feelings. We don't actually have to do something to create it. For instance, if I wish someone dead but don't actually do it, I've still created the energy and the karmic event. Energetically, there is no difference between intending to do it but not actually pulling it off. We can also create karma using our words by lying, misleading someone, by ridiculing or degrading them, or making them suffer. The word, the voice, is the fundamental creative vibration. Moreover, if you think bad thoughts about someone or harbor strong negative feelings about them like hate or anger, these also create karma. Thought and feeling are as powerful as actions, because energetically they actually do create actions, although it takes some time to manifest their effect. When you know this fundamental law of energy, which is that you create with your thoughts, feelings, and desires, you can recreate the most positive effects in your life, or eliminate the most negative ones.

Karma can be healed and balanced in a number of ways. The first of these is through suffering. Many souls come into an incarnation with a plan in which they choose to suffer the same effects as the ones they have caused others. And although an effective way to balance your karma, it requires personal suffering and future lifetimes to accomplish, although it's the only practical way for some. Another way to balance karma is through forgiveness, both by giving and receiving it. If you forgive another for hurting you, you release them from their karma. If you ask another for forgiveness and receive it, this simple act releases you. The original Lord's Prayer did not say "...forgive us our trespasses" but rather, "...forgive us our debts as we have also forgiven our debtors". What the original tells us is that forgiveness is an energy. The basic rule of energy is simple, like attracts like. If one can't forgive, one can't receive forgiveness. This is not because God is holding it back, but rather, because the person is not resonating the energy of forgiveness (in fact the opposite is true), he is unable to attract and receive it. It's our inability to resonate with an energy that prevents us from receiving it.

One can also heal karma through understanding. Many of us operate in life and hurt people without realizing it, or without recognizing the effects of what our actions do to another. When you discover and recognize that something you did actually hurt someone else, that realization can discharge the karma.

The final way to heal karmic imbalance is through God's grace. Never has God's grace been as abundant on earth as it is now. Ask for grace often, and expect to receive it. Oftentimes however, you will be required to process your own karma. You will need to gain the understanding, to ask for forgiveness from the one you hurt, or to forgive the one who has hurt you. I cannot stress enough how powerful or important is the power of forgiveness.

I previously mentioned my mother and what a humble and beautiful person she was. In my entire life, I never heard her say a bad word about anyone, except my father, and then only briefly on two occasions. When my dad was dying of cancer, I spoke with my mom on the phone and told her that it was important for her to forgive him. Somewhat taken aback, she asked, "Charles, why should I forgive him?" My answer was simple. "Mom, it only hurts you if you don't". Please remember this. Harboring bad feelings about anyone hurts you most of all.

CHAPTER TWENTY-TWO

The True Nature and Cause of Illness & Disease

We are not unlucky victims at the mercy of a merciless world. Your health and well-being are a direct result of your thoughts and feelings both in this lifetime, but mostly from past lives. Your thoughts and feelings, whether positive or negative, will reflect themselves in your physical body resulting in good or bad health. Cancer is not a disease. It is a symptom, a symptom of imbalance. Virtually all illnesses are symptoms. The true cause and source of dis-ease or illness are mental and emotional imbalances created by faulty thoughts and emotions that are consistently energized and reinforced, until they ultimately take up residence in the body where they negatively impact the health of your organs and other parts of your physical body. And just as your thoughts and feelings are the source of your bodily ills, you also have the power to heal yourself, by discovering the source of the thoughts and feelings and the circumstances that caused them to happen. Like karma, the imbalances of the body, mind, and emotions can be healed through understanding, grace, forgiveness, and through channeled spiritual energies, which is another form of God's Grace.

In Chapter Sixteen, we talked about the various energy fields or bodies, the Mental, Emotional, and Etheric Bodies which surround the Physical Body. The Physical Body possesses a number of energy centers and distributors that are known as chakras, which means "spinning wheel" in Sanskrit, the sacred language of ancient India. There are a number of these energy centers, each with a different characteristic, role, function, and area of responsibility of the body. The main chakras extend from the base of the spine to the top of the crown of the head, each located about one hand width apart. The chakras act as whirling funnels which draw life force energy into the body. The chakras then redistribute this life force energy, also known as prana, into the physical body. Prana flows consistently through the energy fields and into the chakras which redistribute the prana to the ductless glands, the nervous system, the blood, and ultimately into the organs, tissues, and muscles of the physical body. Without this inflow of prana, none of us would be alive.

Under the best circumstances, this inflow works perfectly. However, the prana must pass through our mental and emotional bodies or energy fields (our thoughts and feelings), prior to entering the chakras and the physical body. The high and pure vibration of the prana is directly affected by the lower vibration of our negative thoughts and feelings which alters and lowers the pranic vibration. The chakra receives the affected prana and spins faster and faster in an attempt to recondition it. If it cannot recondition it, the chakra itself goes out of balance, setting the stage for illness and dis-ease (out of ease). A negative thought or feeling which is constantly reinforced, expressed, or felt consistently will ultimately ride the pranic flow into the body, and take up residence over the organ or body part to which it's related. Moreover, once there, it will impede the energy flow to the organ and confuse the organ over the source of its life force. The confused organ then attempts to take its nourishment from the negative thought or emotion (which it can't) instead of the normal pranic flow. After this breakdown, the disease and its ill effects manifest in and affect the health of the physical body. Although the Physical Body hasn't had a thought or feeling of its own, in effect it takes the hit for the rest of the team.

In order to heal the physical problems caused by negative thoughts and feelings, one must discover the true source of the physical problem, the unbalanced thought or feeling, and heal that. Typically, lifetime after lifetime, people continue to suffer the negative effects of their unbalanced thoughts and feelings until they heal them. The spiritually aware individual is able to enter into altered states of consciousness in which he/she is able to make the connection directly with God and his many helpers, and then to connect with a previous self in a past life, and view and experience the events of that lifetime, and how the faulty thought, unbalanced emotion, or event affects ones current life. Each of us has the ability to heal ourselves, usually with the help of our human and spiritual friends. We also have the ability to help others.

There are many complementary and alternative healing modalities available. At Delphi University we teach a number of them including Color and Sound Healing which restores balance to the chakras, Trance Healing which accesses and channels through the higher spiritual energies, Adult/child therapy, Medical Intuitive, Light Energization™, Reflective Etheric Healing, and many other forms of energy healing. But the most effective energy therapy for healing negative thoughts and unbalanced emotions is the one we pioneered at Delphi called RoHun™ Therapy. There are eleven different individual RoHun™ Therapy processes. Each is extremely effective in permanently healing different aspects of the human psyche. Many say that RoHun™ begins where Carl Jung left off. Unlike conventional medical therapies which attempt to get the personality to explain why they have problems, RoHun™ is a spiritually based therapy which first lifts the person into their higher consciousness. Then they descend into the lower areas of their subconscious and are able to "see" with their spiritual eyes. The healings that are possible through RoHun™ are miraculous and very fast and take from one to four sessions depending on the process. One simple realization can heal the most chronic and challenging mental and emotional problems.

In today's modern world we have the "fix me" attitude. We go for drugs, shots, and surgery, and we look to medicine to heal us. Allopathic medicine is a miracle in itself, one of God's great gifts. Imagine what the world would be without it. But there's more to healing, much more. In many instances, modern medicine cannot find the cure because it's attempting to heal the symptom instead of the cause.

How many of us know someone who was able to heal their cancer, only to have it manifest again months later some-where else in the body? Typically the cancer metastasizes and the person dies soon afterwards. I have also known people with cancer who have had a spiritual renaissance, and whose cancer has never returned. Only by healing the thought or feeling which is the true disease, can one heal the illness and the imbalance.

The responsibility and ability for healing the body, mind, and spirit comes from within. There are seven basic rules or conditions of healing:

1. All illnesses, physical problems and conditions are symptoms, symptoms of imbalance. The physical well-being of a person will be a reflection of their thoughts and feelings.

2. Each person is responsible for their own healing. The "fix me" attitude isn't going to work. Each of us is responsible for ourselves.

3. The individual must truly want to be healed. Many people use their ailments as their purpose for living and being.

4. They must believe that they can be healed. Faith is the prime ingredient for spiritual healing. If one doesn't believe it or at least be open to it, they won't be able to receive it.

5. It must be in their highest interest to be healed. As part of their karmic balancing, many come into life

to suffer. Conceivably, this plan could be altered by the individual if they so choose it.

6. They have to live their lives in a harmonious state. Once healed, they cannot regress to their previous states of thought, feeling, and action, or they will, as fundamentalists often say, "lose their healing".

7. The healing should take place in a conducive place. A dedicated healing room or environment is the best place to perform healings, although you should help someone wherever a need arises.

The physical body is designed according to universal cosmic patterns and responds to violations of cosmic law with disharmony and disease. The negative effects that we experience in life are the result of our own thoughts, feelings, and actions and are a natural energetic consequence and reaction to imbalance, and not the result of God punishing us. When one understands the cause of these imbalances and makes the necessary corrections, changes, and adjustments to these conditions, ill effects disappear, and healing becomes a reality. The process of creation and man's physiology is constantly evolving and unfolding as he heals himself and expresses higher thoughts and feelings. The evolutionary journey of man is the discovery and expression of his true spiritual nature, and the spiritual development of his physical vessel and his subtle bodies, mental, emotional, and etheric.

CHAPTER TWENTY-THREE

The Spiritual Powers & Gifts You Possess

As a child of God, just like your Father/Mother God, you possess many powers. Most of these are unknown to you, and cannot be accessed and developed unless you make a direct connection with your Higher Self. This is accomplished through meditation, the simple act of finding a quiet space for yourself, breathing naturally and rhythmically, and asking your Higher Self to connect with you. It's much like the computer principle of downloading. If you don't make the connection, you can't receive the download.

One of the most fundamental of Universal Laws is that you must ask for what you want. This act is also known as prayer. The Universe will typically support what you ask for, as long as it's in your highest interest, and you are clear in what you request. Unclear, confused, selfish, or indecipherable requests generally yield nothing. In addition, don't try to give the Universe step by step instructions on manifesting what you want. They are much better at it than we are, so let them also do the overall work. Be clear and be consistent in your intentions. Keep asking until it happens. I like to ask for what I can give to others. This is a surefire way to successful invocation.

Divine Self Sufficiency is the source of all of our spiritual abilities. You have a number of powers that you can and do use, many without realizing them. But the great majority of these abilities are unknown or unexpressed by most people. And although these abilities are inherent in every human being to varying degrees, they must be discovered, developed, refined, and expressed. Here's is a list of most of these abilities, but not all of them, in no particular order:

1. The Power of the Word

2. The Power of Thought

3. The Power of Intention

4. The Power of Visualization

5. The Power of Imagination

6. The Power of Manifestation

7. The Power of Invocation

8. The Power of Intuition

9. The Power of the Breath

10. The Power of Healing

11. The Power of Creation

12. The Power of Love

I could not possibly articulate all of the abilities you possess and their myriad aspects. However these are the fundamental gifts of the Divine, and I will explain them as best I can.

> "In the Beginning was the Word, and the Word was with God, and the Word is God" (John 1:1).

This is the very first line from the Book of John which illustrates its significance. One of the most significant of your spiritual abilities is the use of your voice, the *Power of the Word*. The word, or sound vibration, is the fundamental creative energy. It is sound vibration that set off light and color, and it is sound vibration that first caused matter to form, and then to take up regular shapes and patterns to provide for the future life forms that would ultimately be manifested. The word is made manifest in the material worlds. Sound vibration is a also a most significant and powerful healing energy, but also one that can be damaging if used in the wrong way. In human relationships, the power of the word is an energy that should be used wisely and responsibility. Once you say something, it is almost impossible to take it back. The Christ taught that what comes out of your mouth is far more significant than what goes into it. The Buddha taught that, before you say anything to another, ask yourself these three questions: Is it true? Is it necessary? Is it kind? If what one says does not meet these three conditions, it is better left unsaid. Delphi founder Patricia Hayes has demonstrated the power and effect of the word so succinctly in giving us this simple truth:

> "The words I chose create you for me"
> Patricia Hayes

The words I choose create you for me. If I were to tease or berate someone, or tell them they're a no good 'so and so'; within moments I would have created what I said, or would have re-created them into exactly what I said they were. Or if I were to hurt another with my words, chances are good I would have remade them into something far less than what I could have created with positive or even no expression. Even when someone makes a pronouncement like, "I'll never be happy". Their words will create their reality. And once the words are said, no matter what they are, you can't take them back.

Each and every thing and life form that exists is the result of spiritual thought and expression. The material worlds are composed of the thoughts of higher beings, the vibration of which has been stepped down and condensed until they manifest into physical form. God and his many manifestations are thinking the Universe into greater expression and form as you read this. So are you. The *Power of Thought* is the energy that begins and expands everything. A rose is a thought of God (and his children) made manifest. All things begin/began with a thought. God, and each of us, create with our thoughts. Each time you have a thought, you create a conscious, invisible thoughtform whose only purpose is to follow the will of their creator. Idle or random thoughts have little energy and soon dissipate. Strong, reinforced thoughts, particularly those fueled by your emotions and desires, and which are expressed continuously, become active entities which seek out and attract to them energies that are like themselves. Consistency and desire is what differentiates powerful and enduring thoughtforms from their weaker brethren. Your thoughts are the creator of your world and your life.

When you want to create something, you follow your thoughts with the *Power of Intention*. Intention is the act of putting your thoughts into action. Desire is the fuel that energizes intention. When God decided to experience Himself and move into expression, He came out of the void and placed His thoughts into motion. Everything we know is the result of this fundamental activity. In your intention, be clear, be consistent, and be focused. Intention is one of the most powerful forces in the Universe.

To place your intention into motion, you must "image" and visualize what it is you want. These are your next two powers: The *Power of Imagination* and *The Power of Visualization*. I speak of these two in combination, because that's exactly how they work. The imagination is a wonderful energy. Without it, we would still be in the void. Often, when people are waking up to their psychic abilities, they feel like they're making things up. That's because the information comes easily. The imagination is a divine energy that has the same source and comes from the same place as your abilities of clairvoyance (seeing), clairsentience (feeling), and clairaudience (hearing). Look at all the creations in the modern world that have first been imaged or imagined and then have been materialized into form. Once you have imagined something, the next step is to visualize it and fuel it with your desire. If you can "see" or "image" it, you can create it. Your Imagination is a wonderful gift of God. Use it to image and then manifest what you want your life to be.

From these beginnings the *Power of Manifestation* flows. Focus, concentration, and consistency are the engines of manifestation. Clear thoughts, strong desires (particularly spiritual ones), good intentions, and creations based in love are the hallmarks of great manifesters. Combining the power of your thoughts, your imagination, seeing or visualizing what you want, your high and clear intention, and most importantly your love, will result in you becoming a manifestor of the highest order.

As a spiritual being trying to be human, you have many gifts. Often people ask me the question, "Are you Psychic?", to which my reply is, "Yes, aren't you". The puzzled look on some of their faces tells the story. Some people have psychic abilities that just pour out of them. But most people have to develop them. This power, the *Power of Intuition* is inherent in every human being in varying degrees and different levels of development. To see, to feel, to hear, to discern, to know, and to express spiritually is your divine heritage. Many of these abilities were incorporated into your developing physiology during the Ancient Sun phase of our development, long before we arrived on earth.

An adjunct to the power of the word is the *Power of Invocation*. All of us have the power to invoke those higher spiritual energies to assist us with our mission, our purpose, and our expression on earth. To access these spiritual energies you must invoke them or simply ask them to come. This is particularly true when working in healing and helping others. One of the things I do and which we teach at Delphi is invocation using the Divine Names of God in Hebrew. Hebrew is not a language of the earth, but rather, it's a divine language, the vibration of creation. In Hebrew, God is called or named after His attributes of which he has many. But the Hebrew names of God are far more than names; they are divine thoughtforms which, when resonated properly, create and bring through the energy and vibration of the name itself. For instance, the true name of Jesus was Yahoshua which means God or "Yah" delivers. In the Bible, the Christ instructed his followers to "ask anything of the Father in my name and He will give it to you". The name is Yahoshua, which creates the energy or vibration of God delivering to you or me.

As an empowered spiritual being you possess the *Power of Intuition*, the ability to intune or know things that ordinary people can't. Of course, this is a misconception. Everyone has this ability and all of us use it to varying degrees. How many of us have found ourselves in a situation that didn't "feel right", or experienced something that "smelt fishy"; or you just felt uncomfortable in the presence of another. Perhaps you felt that something unknown was going to happen and you "just knew" that it would. Your highest and natural state is that of an all-knowing being. Trust your feelings and "tune in" to the circumstances in your life. Ask your guides and Higher Self to assist you in all you do.

One of the first attributes we developed in our pre-human journey was the ability to breathe. This occurred on Ancient Saturn, and it was a breathing in and out of fire. Air was not yet present. Through this breathing process we were able to project a part of ourselves into matter, creating a duality, of being present both in the physical and in Spirit at the same time. This set the stage for the future incarnation of the human being. On the Ancient Sun we breathed in light and were able to breathe out this light wherever we directed it. Today we use the *Power of the Breath* in all of our spiritual and psychic activities whether that is healing, meditation, psychic readings, counseling, or astral travel. We access these spiritual energy flows, the prana, through our breath. If one wants to make a connection in meditation and enter into altered states of consciousness, one does so through rhythmic breathing. If one wants to bring through information, the information is in the energy, the prana, and is accessed through the breath. So one only has to breathe in with the intention of gaining this information. Through the breath, we can both receive and send energy, even over great distances. Any one of us can be a healer, a reader, a therapist, or a counselor, and channel or bring through the energies of love, light, and healing. We do this once again through intention and the breath.

One simple exercise you can use in everyday life is to breathe in what you want, and breathe out what you don't. For instance, you can breathe in the energy of patience and breathe out impatience, or you can breathe in love and breathe out fear. Just intending to release what doesn't serve your needs and intending to embody what does begins the process of permanent healing. This is an example of how two of your spiritual powers, of breath and intention, can work together. Breathe with intention, and relax when you do it. There's God-Force energy in the breath.

Perhaps one of the greatest gifts bestowed upon man by God is the *Power of Healing*, the power and ability to help others. The Christ told us that we would do greater things than he did, and he actively engaged his disciples in his healing ministry. I have experienced incredible healers, and I have experienced many incredible things myself in my own healing work including healing the sick, raising the dead, and releasing discarnate entities. When you ask to be used as a channel of love, light, and healing, God will use you. In such circumstances you will literally feel the energies coming through you as will the person you are helping. Your hands may become quite hot or even cold. You will find yourself doing things with results you could have only imagined. And you will discover that you have a lot of spiritual helpers working to assist you in your healing work.

When you serve God, God serves you. Every healing is a successful one, even when the person may not receive exactly that for which they asked or expected. A person can receive only what they are able to receive. Even the Christ had many people that weren't ready to receive his love and healing power. But everyone receives something significant in every healing session. The ability to heal ourselves and the contributions of spiritual healers will become more and more significant and essential as this New Day unfolds. Anyone who desires to serve God can ask and receive God's healing energies which they can bring through for the healing of themselves and others. As Patricia Hayes has so eloquently stated:

"The only hands, the only eyes, the only heart that
God has on earth are yours and mine"

Patricia Hayes

199 THE SPIRITUAL POWERS & GIFTS YOU POSSESS

Just like your Father, you have the *Power of Creation*. You are the creator of your life. Most of this happens unwittingly as we are mostly unaware of this fact and how things really work. If there is something you want to create, be clear in your intention. It begins with the energy of Will, the same as God the Father. God creates with His thoughts, and so do you. What follows next is the Plan, the activity of the Christ aspect of God. And then comes the work, the work of the Divine Mother/Holy Spirit of actually bringing things into material form. These are the fundamental steps for manifesting what you want:

1. Decide what it is you want to create and be clear. See and imagine it in your mind's eye.

2. Say what it is you want to create – use the power of the creative word

3. Feel it – feel how much you want it. Let your desire prime the fire.

4. Write it down – this takes your thought and feeling and brings it into physical form.

5. See it complete – In your mind's eye, don't see it coming in stages, but rather see it fully completed.

6. Feel how good it makes you feel to have it completed – this is the fire that fuels the creation

7. Ask for help

8. Do the work – In any plan, your energy is critical to completion. Do anything and everything you can to see it through. God will do his part and you must too.

9. Persevere. Be consistent. Never quit.

10. Give thanks each day for the gifts of God, even for your tests and challenges which help you to discover and become who you really are. Gratitude is the energy that keeps God's gifts flowing to you.

In my business career, I intuitively would do and follow many of these fundamental steps although, at the time, I was mostly unaware of what I was doing. They work even better when you are connected spiritually. You are just like your true parents, a creator of your life and your world.

Finally, I want to talk to you about the one thing that truly matters, for if you access and embody this energy, everything else will fall into place. What I'm talking about is true power, the power of being, of life, of God, the *Power of Love*. There is only love. Everything else is an illusion. All of the energies, all of the powers, all of creation matters not, without love. As the Apostle Paul said so eloquently, "And if I have the gift of prophecy and am acquainted with all the sacred secrets and all knowledge, and if I have all faith so as to remove mountains, but do not have love, I am nothing". The essence of God, the essence of creation, the essence of you is love. Nothing else matters. When you can look into the heart of each and every thing and see there God present, then you will truly know the meaning of love. Love has only one purpose, to fulfill itself. Love has the power to heal, to enlighten, to bring God fully present into the world, and into each of us. Allow your love, God's love, to direct your life and your purpose. Allow your love to flow to others, and most importantly, to yourself. Only in love will you find happiness and peace, and your true Self.

CHAPTER TWENTY-FOUR

And through the darkness, God rediscovers Himself

And through the darkness, God rediscovers Himself. The human journey, the journey to enlightenment and self-realization has progressed for millions of years. All beings, great and small participate in the Divine Plan, the Human Idea. When we were first expressed out of the Godhead we had no sense of self. Only God possessed an Ego. We, His children, had to develop one. The necessary and functional way to start the process is by being selfish, by being totally focused on one's own needs. Selfishness was a necessary part of the plan. Once the ego or little self is established, the task then becomes to evolve it. We develop from stages of selfishness to unselfishness, from taking to giving, from conditional to unconditional love. The goal and purpose of the journey is to first become aware of who and what we really are, second to heal ourselves and overcome those things that keep us from discovering and being who we are, and finally to evolve to our true God-state. God's great gift, your true consciousness, and the purpose of creation is the state of Christ Consciousness, the personality of God. The journey takes us home, back to the heart of love.

In our human journey we live many lifetimes, we make many plans, we go to the places where we can fulfill these plans, and we participate in the Grand Cosmic Drama, the greatest play of all. We enter into expression and there develop the self. Through trial and error, through making mistakes, we discover what we want and what we don't; what's good for us and what isn't. Finally we begin to discover who we really are, and we embark on the path of self-enlightenment. Each of us making the journey should be congratulated, for it isn't easy nor is it for the weak-hearted. What does an eternal being do with eternity and an unlimited source of energy? When we ultimately return to Oneness, we are far different then when we first embarked on our journey, for we are now the Self-aware, the Ego-bearers, little Gods serving the Big God, different but the same as the one who first expressed us, fully aware and fully Christ Conscious. What do we gain from the journey? In addition to our experience, we gain the greatest gift of all, the gift of Self, our God selves, fully aware, fully awake, fully empowered, at the same time individuals and yet a part of the whole. We are many, yet we are one.

Along the way, God gives us many gifts, everything we need to figure out who we are and to become what we are. In addition to Divine Self Sufficiency, we receive the gifts of Birth, Life, Death, and Rebirth. We get to play many roles, wearing many garbs, assuming many faces, living in many different places. We have as many experiences and as many lifetimes as we need to "get it right". We are provided with the energy and the resource of Time, the time in which to act and to change our minds. And we are provided with Space, that physical phenomena which allows for movement and change. We are given these incredible bio computers known as the Mind which allows us to think, to reason, to make choices, and to develop an ego or sense of self. Additionally we are restricted by the Forces of Resistance, which provide obstacles from which we learn and as a counter to Divine Self Sufficiency. God gives us everything we need to discover who we truly are and to evolve into the state of God/Christ Consciousness.

God will never force you to do something nor will he ever punish you. God loves you completely and knows that each of us will eventually find our way back home, because we are just like Him, with all his gifts, powers, and abilities. He also knows and experiences everything you feel because He is you. Your Higher Self is the director and planner of your life. With each difficulty that comes in life, there is also a gift and a purpose. Look for it. Know too that for each problem, each challenge you have planned, you have also brought the solution as well. From a spiritual perspective in human affairs, almost nothing is what it seems. Don't be too quick to judge an event. There is hidden meaning in all things. Look for the hidden meaning and the gift in everything, in every aspect of your life. God brings the unexpected. Also understand that the new cannot come in until the old has departed. Oftentimes when you lose you gain. Know that you are loved, supported, and watched over continuously. If you want what's real, you'll have to give up what isn't.

Many of us have been disenchanted or disappointed by our religion. Religions are but a glimpse of the whole truth, and most religions claim exclusive access to God. Once a visionary brings through spiritual truth, his disciples immediately build walls around it, codify and dogmatize it, and eliminate all other perspectives, thus preventing any more spiritual wisdom from coming through. Spiritual wisdom itself is a continuation of all that has come before. There's a fundamental difference between spirituality and religion. In spirituality you know things because you feel and experience them, and not just because you were told to believe them. And yet, if a belief system works for someone, it works. Who am I or anyone to dictate what a person should or shouldn't do, or how they should experience life or interact with God? Each of us must discover our own path, in the way we are most able, and then choose to follow it or not. The evolutionary journey of man is the discovery and expression of his true spiritual nature, and the spiritual development of his physical vessel and subtle bodies. The Christ Energy has already returned within the hearts and the minds of mankind. Don't look for him to descend from the clouds, but rather, look for this energy to unfold within you.

If you would be whole, if you would like to fulfill your true and greatest potential, then you will follow the path of enlightenment. There's a whole new and incredible world waiting for you if you do. To enter upon the spiritual path, you simply have to set your intention and desire to discover who and what you really are, and ask God for help. You have many spiritual guides and helpers that will assist you. A spiritually aware person can enter into altered states of consciousness and have direct experience, communication, and connection with God and his many helpers. You will be overjoyed at all you will experience and become along the way. You will empower yourself to direct your own life, instead of life directing you. And once you unfold and experience yourself spiritually, you will find it hard to go back to what you once were. But the journey or the Path is not for the weak-minded or the faint of heart, for you will also be tasked to discover and heal those mental and emotional blocks and energies that hold you back. A spiritually aware person is required to do more and to be more. In the words of my precious wife Kimberly, "You can only go as high as you are willing to go low".

You will also experience setbacks along the way. Just when you feel you're making progress, something will happen in your life that will stop you in your tracks. This is known as a setback. But a setback is really a setup, because you can't be setback unless you are moving forward, and a setback is proof that you are moving. View setbacks as learning opportunities which enable you to gather and collect yourself and move forward with a renewed vigor and perspective. And remember, God never gives you more than you can handle, and if he does, he rescues you. In my own journey God has rescued me more than once.

For those we call Initiates, for those who would embark along the path of self-realization, awareness, and enlightenment, there are some simple things you can do:

1. Act like you know what you're doing. This is the fundamental spiritual instruction. For, from a spiritual

perspective, you actually do.

2. Second, you must ask for help and for what you need. If you don't ask, you won't receive it. This is universal law.

3. Develop the energy of love. Breathe love in and send love out. Each day, think of someone you love or who needs love, and send your love to them. Then feel your love of God, and God's love for you. And don't neglect to love and honor yourself.

4. Dedicate time each day for your spiritual practice. Meditate. Read. Give yourself a few minutes of quiet time a day to just breathe, connect with God, and receive the gifts of Spirit.

5. Be open to new things and new experiences. Connect with like-minded people. Take a class or a workshop. Develop your spiritual understanding. Empower yourself.

6. Pay attention to your thoughts and feelings, especially negative ones. If you don't energize or act on them when they rise, they will fall quickly and weaken over time.

7. Treat others as you would like to be treated. Choose your words carefully and with love. Don't judge others or yourself.

8. See God in all things, particularly in people, especially when they're suffering and giving you a hard

time. Know that they are on their own path and are trying to work things out, just as we all are. Be sensitive to them and to yourself.

9. Share your goodness. A smile, a greeting, a kind word, or a considerate act are simple gifts of love and healing that you can share with others. The essence of God is goodness.

10. Trust that the Universe is with you and will direct your course and your progress. As God told me when first I asked; "You will know everything when it is time".

It is inevitable that, sooner or later, all human beings will follow the Path of Christ Consciousness and Self-awareness. It's our birthright and our destiny. In ancient times God spoke to man from the outside. In the New Day, God speaks from within. The child, in becoming spiritually empowered and aware, progresses until ultimately he becomes the father, an awakened, aware, and empowered Christ Conscious Human Being. Not perfect, but whole. As the Christ said so simply, "I and the Father are One". If you go deep within your own heart and strip away all the layers and all the crust, there you will find Him.

Know Thyself. Living in the New Day means becoming who and what you really are. Let your Higher Self direct your purpose, and let your human desire body become the Desire Body of God. Know that in life, if you are doing something that helps others and is also something which you enjoy, then you have found your purpose. Find your purpose and fulfill it. The ultimate purpose of life is to love and to give yourself to Self purpose. To love is to serve God. Anyone who desires to serve God need only to ask for His love and healing, and He will answer. Ask to be used, and God will use you. And don't be afraid. Know that you are worthy. Trust that God loves and honors you, will provide for you, and only wants the best for you. You are a child of God, and God loves you dearly. And know, without any doubt, that God never leaves his sons and daughters behind. Even now He waits for you, with arms wide open, and a smile in His Heart.

So that's my story, all of it true. One day in October became a New Day for me. Today, this day, if you choose it to be so, is a New Day for you. It is my fervent hope and desire that you will discover and follow your path, the path of self-discovery and self-awareness, the path of love, and the way back home to the Heart of God. I send my love and my prayers to you each day to help you along the way. May the blessings of the One Most High be with you and keep you always.

Delphi University
Of Spiritual Studies

Delphi University is a world-renowned school of spiritual training, energy healing, metaphysics, holistic healing, esoteric & self-enlightenment studies, transpersonal psychology, psychic training, and intuitive development. Equally important, Delphi is also a magical place of personal growth, healing, and self-realization, a beautiful spiritual retreat center dedicated to the healing of body, mind, and spirit. Founded by Patricia Hayes in 1974, Delphi is the place for those seeking to Discover, Develop, Refine and Express their Spiritual Gifts and Abilities, as well as to Grow, Transform, and Heal themselves.

For over 35 years Delphi University has been a leader in the fields of spiritual training, alternative and complementary healing, psychic and intuitive development, and personal self-empowerment. The combination of our unique and experiential training programs, our exceptional staff of instructors and healers, each of who has decades of spiritual

210

practice and experience, the beautiful natural environment here, and the high spiritual energies that operate at Delphi allow students to accelerate their spiritual development and their personal growth and healing, as well as having deep and meaningful spiritual experiences, as they learn, grow, and develop. Delphi is a unique experience, and a place we all call home.

We welcome and invite you to discover and develop your true and greatest potential here at Delphi. You will gain a greater awareness and understanding about Self and Spirit, more fully and reliably develop your spiritual gifts and abilities, and learn to bring healing to yourself and others. If you would like to know more about Delphi University and our certification programs, and how to enrich your life as a spiritual healer, intuitive counselor, life coach, and/or spiritual psychotherapist, please contact us:

Delphi University - of Spiritual Studies

940 Old Silvermine Rd, PO Box 70

McCaysville, GA 30555

Toll Free 1-888-335-7448

Email: registrar@delphiu.com

Website: www.delphiu.com

The Secrets of my Business Success

Over the years I have been asked to share the secrets of my entrepreneurial success. Now I would like to share them with you:

1. Take a Chance – Look for an opportunity and go for it, for you never know what you can do until or unless you try.

2. Work Hard – There is simply no substitute for hard work. Those that work hard succeed. Those who don't fail.

3. Do what feels right – Many a great decision has been made solely on the basis that it felt like the right thing to do.

4. Do the Best you can – In life, all that anyone can ask of you, or you can ask of anyone is to do your best.

5. Make the Best Use of Your God-Given Abilities – We all have different talents and abilities. Use your own potential to its' fullest.

6. Have Fun – Hard work and fun are not exclusive of each other. It you don't enjoy what you do, you'll never be happy.

7. Use Your Luck/Make the Best of Your Opportunities – I often find that the harder I work, the luckier I get.

8. Form a clear mental idea of what you want to create. Visualize it. Imagine it. Say it. Write it down. See it already completed in your mind's eye, and feel how good that makes you feel. Ask for help from the Divine. Do the above steps often. Last but not least, you must do the work.

Finally and most importantly.....

9. Persevere – No matter how tough the going gets, or how impossible the odds seem or become, hang in there. In the early days of my business career I often wanted to quit, to give up. If you quit you lose, but if you refuse to quit, you're still in the game and you can still win. Unlike sporting events, there is no game clock, time limit, or shot clock. Perseverance is truly the quality that separates the women from the girls and the men from the boys, and the key ingredient for success.